EDUCATING THE MEXICAN CHILD

IN THE ELEMENTARY SCHOOL

by

Katherine Hollier Meguire

A Thesis

University of Southern California

1938

Reprinted in 1973 by R and E Research Associates,
4843 Mission Street, San Francisco, California
94112 and 18581 McFarland Avenue, Saratoga,
California 95070

Publishers and Distributors of Ethnic Studies
Editor: Adam S. Eterovich
Publisher: Robert D. Reed

Library of Congress
Card Catalog Number
73-78056

ISBN 0-88247-231-3

TABLE OF CONTENTS

CHAPTER I
THE PROBLEM

The purpose of this study is to present methods and procedures that may be employed in the elementary schools in coping with the major problems that confront teachers of Mexican children. It is hoped that the methods and practices presented here will aid teachers of Mexican children, particularly the beginning teachers who are thrust into a situation for which they have no background of understanding, to achieve more readily and more effectively their goal, that of guiding these Mexicans in becoming happy, successful, contributing members of American society.

I. NEED FOR THE STUDY

Every year great numbers of teachers, totally unprepared for their coming job, are suddenly faced with the task of teaching Mexican children in the elementary grades.

They have no knowledge of the Mexican race, of its characteristics, or of its ideals; and they, therefore, must grope blindly for an understanding of these people and of the problems to be met in their education, before they can achieve any kind of success toward their goal. In the meantime they cause, far more often than they remedy, maladjustments to environment and society, and utterly fail in the end to educate these Mexican children.

These teachers need to learn methods that have been successfully employed in the teaching of Mexicans, and reasons for these methods, so that they can use in their own schoolrooms the most efficient ways of reaching their goals.

The writer in a diligent search was unable to locate a comprehensive presentation of such methods. It is, therefore, her desire to compile for the use of these teachers techniques to bring about the best results in the education of Mexican children.

II. NATURE OF EXISTING CONDITIONS

According to reports presented on the census of 1930, there were then 1,422,533 Mexicans in the United States,[1] and it is safe to say that this number has not decreased appreciably since that time. The vast majority of them are concentrated in the four southwestern states bordering upon Old Mexico. Their education becomes the duty of the schools in these states.

However, as these Mexican people are of a race whose customs, characteristics, and ideals are different from our own, they present many problems different from those met in the education of American children.

Furthermore, the larger percentage of these Mexicans belong to the lower strata of society, even in Mexico. They are the peons, the unskilled labor class. It is this class that presents the greatest educational problems to the public schools, and it is this class with which the present study concerns itself.

A brief presentation of the historical background, of the economic social status, and of the personality of the Mexicans in the United States with which this study concerns itself will throw further light on the nature of and need for the study.

Even though the Mexicans in the life of many of the Southwestern states have become too numerous to ignore, and even though they present a great problem to many school systems, there exist practically no pre-service training schools or courses for teachers who are to become educators of the Mexican children.

These teachers, products of an American culture, fresh from American teacher-training institutions, steeped in American theories and practices, suddenly find themselves confronted with the baffling problem of teaching an entirely different race of people whose speech, thoughts, characteristics, and ideals are so very different from their own. They are overwhelmed by the task and begin to seek answers to such questions as: "Why are the Mexicans here in such numbers? What are their ideals and characteristics? How do they live? What is their greatest handicap? How do Americans feel toward them? How can their teachers best serve them?"

It is hoped that the following brief answers to all but the last of the above questions will give these teachers a background of understanding and a basis from which to proceed in utilizing the suggested methods contained in the body of this writing. These suggested methods are the collective answer to the final question in the list.

<u>Why are the Mexicans here in such numbers?</u> A many-fold answer can be given to this question. In the past when the bars of immigration were down, they flocked in to make their homes in a country which seemed to offer advantages and remunerations far in excess of anything they could hope for in their own land. During the many periods of rebellion and unrest that Mexico has suffered in the past few years, many more of her people came to the United States to seek the safety they could not find in Mexico. However, the chief reason why so many are here is because they are the "cheap labor" that the industrialists in any community cry for. They have been imported by the thousands to save the capitalists' money. The communities themselves use great numbers of them for the most lowly and servile labors that necessarily must be performed in the course of every day living.

In many sections of the South and West there exist employment agencies that represent organizations such as Michigan beet farmers, Pennsylvania coal mine owners, cotton farmers, fruit and vegetable growers, or pecan shelling plants. These employment agencies find in the Mexicans the solution to their problem of cheap seasonal and itinerant labor, so they use means, fair or foul, of getting them into the United States and of keeping them here.

This brings up a point which many people are unwilling to recognize. When confronted with the "Mexican problem," many of them say, "Send them back to Mexico. That is where they belong." They quite lose sight of the fact that a great majority of these Mexicans are born citizens of the United States and are here to stay. They cannot be dismissed with an impatient exclamation and wave of the hand toward Mexico. Instead, they must be molded into worthwhile citizens of our nation; and in this work, the schools must lead the way.

What are their ideals and characteristics? Their ideals and characteristics are outgrowths of their race history. The Mexican does not come of purebred stock. His race is a mixture of the Aztec Indians who achieved a Montezumian form of culture and of the fiery-blooded Spanish conquistidores who conquered Mexico to intermingle with its natives and impose their Old World Culture upon them.

Mexican ideas are very different from our own. The Mexicans have ambition for a leisurely life that is an outgrowth of their ancestry. The conquerors of Mexico were not some of the laboring class in Spain, but were some of Spain's great feudal families who saw life in terms of danger mastered and of riches accumulated without work. Even in the Aztec culture, the warrior was lauded and the worker was degraded. Work was considered demeaning by both the invader and the vanquished. They sought pleasure and happiness in leisure. Eva A. Frank,[2] in writing about Mexico, says that a man's ambition there is to collect enough money, not to set himself up in business so that he can make more money, but so that he can retire and enjoy life.

With the Spanish invasion there were imposed upon the inhabitants of Mexico many of the Spanish customs and habits of thought which in part explain marked characteristics in the Mexicans of today. For example, the strong love for color and beauty is easily seen in the native dress of both nations, in the works of art they produce, and in the brilliant decorations used in national spectacles such as bullfights and fiestas. The Spanish and Mexican delight in rhythm is well-known, and their music and dances have long been enjoyed throughout the world.

Wherever Spanish influence has held sway, other characteristics are very noticeable. Spanish dominance has made followers of the people, who developed traits of irresponsibility and a submission to authority that is sure death to initiative and self-dependence.

The Spanish custom of chaperonage and separation of the sexes, together with a latitude and climate that bring on early maturity, have made the Mexican people highly sex-conscious, a trait displayed even by little six- and eight-year-old children.

The latitude and climate are also partly responsible for another easily detected characteristic, that of procrastination. The habit of languidly putting off until manana the duties of today is very irksome to many Americans whose thoughts and actions are geared up to a higher pitch.

Still another characteristic with which the schools must deal is that of individualism. Cooperative enterprises, ranging all the way from well-established political parties to nationally-loved games requiring teamwork, are lacking in the Mexican national life.

Teachers armed with a knowledge of such characteristics as described here will be better able to cope with the problems presented by their little Mexican pupils.

How do they live? Manuel answers this question in the following description of the Mexicans in one of the four states bordering Mexico, and other writers have indicated that like conditions are common in the other states as well.

> Typically, except in the most favorable situations, the Mexican element of a community lives in a section or sections to itself. 'Across the tracks' and 'Little Mexico' are phrases full of meaning to hundreds of Texas communities. In these sections Mexicans tend to preserve their language and customs. While the housing conditions vary widely, the average is far below that of the section of the community occupied by other whites. At the lowest end of the scale are conditions indescribably poor, and with them the usual train of attendant evils--overcrowding, undernourishment, disease, superstition, filth, and social maladjustment. No description is adequate for the person who has not seen such conditions close at hand.[3]

Lanigan, in a study of Mexicans in a certain section of California, paints a similar picture, naming one of the deplorable results--crime.

> There is scant inspiration in their homes; their mothers are slaves to huge families; their fathers are out of work; they themselves are sometimes hungry. They have no smart clothes, no money for pleasure. They look about them and see hundreds of others in a similar situation. They see stealing as a short cut to pleasure and excitement. It is small wonder that they take it.[4]

Many pages could be filled with such quotations and with first-hand descriptions of conditions, but these two, plus an observant study of the children before her, should suffice in giving the teacher the information she seeks about the way they live and in suggesting to her many goals toward which she may aim in helping them to improve their conditions.

What is their greatest handicap? Undoubtedly the greatest one is language. Possessed of this all-important key, they can find ways to lessen the others to a great degree. With the ability to think, speak, and read English will come opportunities for more remunerative employment, and with that, ways to improve their home environment, which is the collective term for most of the other handicaps.

However, in trying to give the Mexicans this ability to use English fluently, the schools meet with one of their most perplexing problems. The Mexicans live in close-knit colonies; they are rarely accepted as equals by Americans, so they follow the customs of their own people, speak their own language, and teach their children to do the same. They are a proud race and seem to feel ridicule very keenly, so they will often deny knowledge of English rather than attempt to speak it and run the risk of being laughed at.

These conditions make it necessary for the teacher to seek and to use those methods and procedures which have been found to be most successful during the past years of experimentation on the teaching of English to Mexican children.

How do Americans feel toward them? In the communities most vitally concerned, widely divergent thoughts on this point are found. In some sections the Mexicans are accepted as a matter of course, and are considered social equals with the shites at the various levels of society which naturally exist.

However, this state does not seem to typify the feeling in general. In far too many instances the Mexicans are treated as inferiors, discriminated against, and scorned as equals even though many of them belong to the upper strata of society in Mexico.

Much of the literature concerning Mexicans in the United States contains accounts of the unfavorable attitude of Americans toward them, of Mexican children being barred from schools, or of their being provided with inferior equipment and poorly-trained teachers because of their nationality.

Innumerable personal experiences could be recounted to illustrate further this attitude of superiority and contempt with which the Mexican is regarded by unthinking and uninformed Americans. For example, one teacher (a stranger to the writer) not concerned with the education of any non-English-speaking children, casually inquired the subject of this thesis, and when told, remarked, "Who cares what we do about teaching the Mexican children anyway?" This so typifies the ignorance of, and feeling about, the education of Mexicans and other racial groups.

How can their teachers best serve them? Bogardus, in his excellent study of the Mexicans in this country, says, "The Mexican child needs nothing so much as to be understood by men and women of deep human sympathy."[5] Rodee amplifies this same thought. She says:

> All instruction to these children needs a large sympathy and deep understanding of human nature, the gospel measure of patience, and an interest that knows no faltering . . . . There should be a feeling of comradeship, friendliness and mutual belief in each other between pupil and teacher, in order that the child may be freed of every embarrassment and of self-consciousness and brought into perfect harmony and accord with the teacher's leadership and purposes.[6]

In addition to these fine qualities, the teacher also needs a knowledge of methods and procedures which are best suited to the Mexican child. It is hoped that material set forth in the body of this study will supply these needs and will do much to aid the teachers of Mexican children in understanding and in instructing their pupils so that these boys and girls may attain the most worthy goals toward which all education aims.

III. EXPLANATION OF TERMS

Mexican. The term "Mexican" as used in this study refers to those people who descend from, or who were the native inhabitants of present Mexico. Thousands of "Mexicans" are born in the United States and technically are citizens of this country, but in reality they are as truly Mexican as are their parents and other ancestors.

American. The term "American" as used in this study refers to the people who are as truly the products of the culture of this nation as the Mexicans are of Mexico.

America. The term "America" as used in this study refers to the United States of America.

IV. LIMITATIONS OF THE STUDY

This study attempts to present methods that the elementary classroom teacher can use in the school. It does not expect that she as merely a teacher will have the power to bring about changes in administration or organization other than to receive the cooperation of her associates.

It invades the realm of the social worker, the social environment outside the school, only so far as the teacher from her post can have influence there.

No attempt is made to evaluate the methods here given, or to recommend them as the only possible ones. Their value lies in the fact that they have been used successfully by teachers of Mexican children and are applicable in some instances if not in all.

FOOTNOTES

[1] "Special Report on Foreign-born White Families by Country of Birth of Head," Fifteenth Census of the United States: 1930. Population. (United States Dept. of Commerce. Bureau of the Census. Washington: U.S. Govt. Printing Office, 1933), p. 199.

[2] Eva A. Frank, "The Mexican 'Just Won't Work,'" Nation, 125:156, 8, 1927.

[3] H. T. Manuel, The Education of Mexican and Spanish-Speaking Children in Texas (The Fund for Research in the Social Sciences, Austin: The University of Texas, 1930), p. 18.

[4] Mary Lanigan, "Second Generation Mexicans in Belvedere," (unpublished Master's thesis, University of Southern California, Los Angeles, 1932), p. 68.

[5]E. S. Bogardus, <u>The Mexican in the United States.</u> (Los Angeles: The University of Southern California Press, 1934), p. 159.

[6]Nona Rodee, <u>Teaching Beginners to Speak English.</u> (Tucson, Arizona: Tucson Public Schools, 1923), p. 15.

CHAPTER II
THE PROCEDURE

The procedure followed in the preparation of this study may be divided into three phases. Difficulties met by teachers of Mexican children were listed and classified, then methods were sought to overcome the major problems that evolved from this classification. The third phase was the classification and compilation of these methods in the form of suggestions to the teacher of Mexican children.

I. LISTING THE DIFFICULTIES

First, with a desire to write something that would help teachers of the elementary grades to understand and more effectively teach Mexican children, the writer listed all the difficulties she had encountered or could think of in this connection on small slips of paper, each an eighth of a sheet of typewriter paper in size. Each difficulty was phrased in the "How to do something" style, and each was written at the top of a separate slip. Literature on the subject of teaching Mexicans was skimmed for additional difficulties and these, too, were added to the pile.

These slips were sorted into stacks according to type of difficulty presented on each. It was found that there were three main divisions; educational, psychological, and sociological problems, in the teaching of Mexican children.

It was then necessary to analyze more closely the difficulties and to discard such ones as applied to nearly all teaching situations. Only those that were peculiarly Mexican, or that had to be more stressed with Mexican children than with American children were retained.

The final grouping arrived at was under the following main headings:

1.   How to teach spoken English to Mexican children.

2. How to teach the reading of English to Mexican children.

3. How to combat the common condition of poor health among Mexicans.

4. How to deal with racial traits displayed by Mexican children.

5. How to establish a feeling of equality with Americans.

6. How to meet the needs of Mexican boys and girls at upper elementary levels.

II. COLLECTING THE METHODS

The second phase of the work consisted of searching for methods that had been used by workers among Mexicans to overcome the difficulties listed. This was done in two ways.

First, all printed material on the subject available to the writer was located through the use of various indexes and bibliographies and searched for explanations of the difficulties and ways to overcome them. Notes were taken on similar slips to those mentioned above, each idea or method on a separate slip.

Second, the writer personally visited and interviewed administrators, teachers, and social workers who have had experience in educating Mexican children. She also interviewed administrators and teachers of American schools in order to have a basis for comparison in selecting methods used or more stressed in the teaching of Mexican children.

Several excellent opportunities for these contacts presented themselves. One was the discussion groups and the private interviews held with various summer school students of the University of Southern California. As these students represented many sections of the country, the writer was able to check her list of difficulties and methods for overcoming them for universality and discard those which seemed peculiar to individual localities.

Another fruitful sourse of information was found in two night school classes which drew their enrollments from the elementary schools of a city which rates approximately sixty-two percent of its elementary children as Mexican. Here the writer was able to compare problems found in Mexican and American schools and retain in her list those difficulties and methods which applied more specifically to the Mexican children.

Still another source was the demonstration classes held each term in schools throughout the writer's own school system. These demonstrations are for the purpose of acquainting teachers with approved methods. They are held during the school day and are actual classroom situations. The writer was permitted to leave her own class and attend several of these demonstrations in both American and Mexican schools. In this way, much excellent material was gathered.

A fourth source was the writer's own school, rated Mexican, which is under the directorship of Miss Elma Neal, an outstanding authority on the development of methods and procedures for the education of the Mexican child.

All suggestions obtained were recorded on slips to be classified under the main headings which had been decided upon.

III. CLASSIFYING THE METHODS

The third phase of the work consisted of classifying and catalogueing the methods collected under the six major problems.

As the work progressed, the slips were sorted frequently in order to arrive at tentative outlines under each main grouping. The limitations of the study, how the teacher from her classroom post of duty could overcome the major problems met in the education of elementary Mexican children, was constantly kept in mind to guide the selection and organization of methods. Those which depended upon some peculiar classroom set-up not met in the average school were discarded, as were those which pertained to teaching in general rather than teaching Mexican children in particular. An effort was made to present only those methods which could be used in almost any classroom of Mexican pupils, whether it be in a one-room country school, or in a school in a city system.

Each of these major problems is so interrelated with the others that some trouble was experienced in classifying several of the methods. Therefore, it was decided to use some methods in more than one chapter as means of achieving different ends. This material was then presented in the form of explanations and suggestions for use by teachers of Mexican children.

I. EMPLOY THE DIRECT METHOD

The direct method in learning a language has been compared to the touch system in learning typing. It seems slow at first, but with usage it becomes easier and easier.[2]

The advantages of this method over the others, the translation and the natural methods, must be clearly understood. The translation method, as its name implies, uses the native tongue as a basis and attempts to fit foreign words to native-formed ideas. This sets up the necessity of an intermediate step in the mind. The thought is formed in one language, then the student must search his memory for the words and word orders of the new language in order to express his thought. It seldom has the true ring of the language because of the necessary double shift made in the mind. Thought and expression processes are slowed down, and it requires an enormous amount of study and practice before the student is able to use the new language with ease.

The so-called natural method is not a method at all. It is just the haphazard acquisition of a foreign language through contact and practice with those to whom the language is native.

The direct method also teaches through contact and practice but the instruction is carefully planned and logically organized so that the pupil may proceed in orderly fashion to build concepts and thought expression in terms of his new language without resorting to his old, and with the greater degree of facility that accompanies a well-planned undertaking.

Since the teacher's aim and the purpose of the direct method--to establish habits of thinking and expression in a new language--coincide, she will find the following suggestions helpful with her Mexican children.

Set the children at ease. Provide them with toys, games, pictures, and pleasant pasttimes in order to form a favorable attitude toward this strange English world into which they have been thrust. No Spanish words will be spoken to them, and they will not be encouraged to speak in their language to others, so they must be given no time to feel fright. The teacher can begin laying her firm groundwork this very first day by having the children participate in some exercise, as a flag salute, and imitate a short English sentence or two even if they do not comprehend.

In almost every class there will be found a few children with some slight knowledge of English. The teacher can discover the extent of these children's skill and use it in little games to make the use of English seem fun.

Much praise and many rewards in privileges to those who attempt English will establish an encouraging atmosphere and will help to overcome the Mexican's timidity.

Pleasant little stories full of gestures and actions that help him to comprehend the words will lessen the feeling of strangeness toward English.

In short, the Mexican child must be made to feel at home and familiar with a little world that is in reality very strange to him.

Choose beginning vocabulary for immediate use. The Mexican child must be reintroduced to himself and his environment in terms of a new language. The universal, basic principle of teaching or learning is to proceed from the known to the unknown. Therefore, the best known and most frequently used ideas and objects are the ones the teacher chooses for use first in teaching English.

A subject vitally important to the children, such as their own identity, is used first in introducing English in a conversational way. For example, the teacher says very distinctly to a child, "I am Miss Jones. Who are you?" She helps him to reply, "I am Juan." Around the circle she goes, using the same procedure. So the light of comprehension shines in many faces as names of little friends are heard at the end of the unfamiliar words, and the children begin to "catch on" to the little game.

Thus English is begun, and day by day the means to express other thoughts about themselves or their surroundings are added to the children's knowledge. It is essential that this core vocabulary be made up of words of such common use that the children are sure to use them again and again in expressing their immediate needs.

Use concrete materials. This is an essential feature of the direct method of instruction. One authority clearly states the thought of many teachers of Mexican

II. DEVELOP AUDITORY RECOGNITION AND PRONUNCIATION

Not a small part of the teacher's efforts to teach Mexican children to speak English must be directed toward training their ears to hear sounds correctly and their tongues to reproduce those sounds in rapid succession to form English words.

If the child can acquire the ability to hear correctly and make himself understood with ease in his new language, his whole personality will adjust more easily to the strange English world.

Too often Mexicans poorly trained in oral language are thought to be stupid simply because they are too timid or self-conscious to speak and be forced to repeat several times what they have tried to convey.

Below are some ways in which the teacher can help her Mexican children to hear and to speak English clearly, and correctly.

Speak slowly. To the foreign ear, the language is only a series of unintelligible sounds. These sounds must be spoken slowly enough so that familiar ones may be recognized. It is well to speak to Mexican children in short sentences, and to phrase carefully, hesitatingly slightly at the end of each group of words so that they have time to catch the sound combinations and comprehend them.

Rapid speech forms bad habits. The children's minds cannot keep pace, so they give up listening entirely and simply wait for the flow of words to cease. It is quite beyond their power to imitate such rapid speech, so they form the habit of not trying.

The teacher must speak slowly and distinctly, but she must be careful to preserve the proper inflections and expression if she expects her children's English to sound natural.

Use, and insist upon, clear enunciation. The common habit of slurring words is one which the teacher must overcome in herself very quickly if she wishes to obtain clear-cut sounds from her Mexican pupils. It is far better to over-emphasize word sounds than to neglect them.

Listen for the endings of words. Mexicans are prone to neglect "es"s, "ed"s, and "ly"s. Watch the child's mouth to see that he is saying "vacation" and not "bacation." Avoid contractions, lest the child will fall into this habit before he is ready to use it. Never forget that the child learns through imitation and that he will reflect the speech habits, good and bad, of his teacher.

Stress letter sounds and phonograms. This work with Mexican children is very important in ear and speech training, and is often continued into the upper elementary grades. Many little games and rhymes can be used by the teacher to make this necessary drill pleasant.

Use "visible speech" methods. This type of work should have a place in the daily program throughout the lower elementary grades. The teacher must demonstrate the placement of the vocal organs, exaggerating the movements, so they can be easily seen and imitated. She must not trust to hearing entirely, either the child's or her own, to insure the correct reception and reproduction of sounds.

Concentrate drills upon pronunciation difficulties. Throughout the grades the teachers will find numbers of Mexican children displaying the same pronunciation difficulties. These children should be grouped according to difficulty and have language games and drills devised to overcome their special trouble. For example, the letter "j" is given an "h" sound in Spanish. In English this letter sound is sometimes difficult for Mexican children to pronounce. A little game that can be used for drill on this sound follows. A child says, "Miss Jennie J. Jones journeyed to Jericho and what did she see (or do)?" He then calls on children who must reply with words beginning with "j", such as, "She saw some jars." or "She jumped a rope." Other letters or phonograms that need to be emphasized with the group can replace the "j" words in the replies to vary the game and supply other necessary drill.

Use choric speaking sparingly. It is said that concert speaking lends confidence to the timid and does much toward developing expression in the voice. However, with Mexican children it also gives much opportunity to form careless or incorrect pronunciation habits. Therefore, the teacher must be certain that correct individual speech habits are firmly established before she allows her Mexican pupils to participate in much choric speaking.

III. PROVIDE OPPORTUNITIES FOR THE USE OF ENGLISH

It cannot be stressed too strongly to teachers of Mexican children that they are primarily teachers of language. Oral work with these children is paramound, and subject-matter must be subordinated to it.

Mrs. Rodee, in her instructions to teachers of Mexican children says,

> Teacher, remember you are teaching <u>language</u> . . . . remember you are not teaching dancing as an <u>art,</u> no more than you are teaching drawing or sewing as an art. You are simply correlating these activities with English for the sake of <u>English.</u>[4]

The teacher must be ever on the alert to provide pleasant ways for the children to use English. Many of them dislike to talk because of the great effort required to express themselves in a foreign language. Others are fearful that they will make mistakes and will be ridiculed. Therefore, the stimuli offered must be powerful enough to overcome these reluctancies.

<u>Use many language games.</u> Little action games in which children try to describe their movements without a mistake or in which one must describe the movements of another are always enjoyed. Such games develop thinking in English and make for facility of expressions.

<u>Have personal experience conversations.</u> These are so profitable for both teacher and pupil. The teacher gains valuable information about the child's strange Mexican environment, and the child learns to express his thoughts about situations that are entirely outside the school setting. The element of interest will carry the child through many language difficulties he would be unwilling to attempt in teacher-made situations.

<u>Organize an oral newspaper.</u> A large number of children can participate in this activity. They can be organized into the various sections of a newspaper, and each can contribute items of interest in his particular section. The weekly or bi-weekly visits of such a newspaper are looked forward to with much interest by other rooms in the school, and they give valuable oral experience to the participants.

<u>Use many short units and projects.</u> In unit and project work, vocabulary can

be more firmly implanted in the mind than in unrelated subject teaching. Many short units are better than one or two long ones for several reasons. The children's interest is restimulated; they gain a wider vocabulary; they are given opportunity for more oral work in the form of unit summaries (possibly performed as auditorium programs); and they develp more leisure time interests for outside pursuance.

Develop skill in story-telling. This practice will help the Mexican child to coordinate a series of thoughts in English. Even allowing the child to repeat a memorized story has its advantages. It gives him confidence in speaking, and helps him to produce a smooth flow of English words.

Use many pictures and objects for descriptions. This concrete teaching is one of the primary principles of the direct method of instruction in English. The pictures and objects furnish a never-ending source of subjects for oral work. Many little games can make this work very interesting. For instance, a child is told the name of a familiar picture. If he can clearly describe a certain number of points in the picture, he wins it for the time being. At the end of the game, the one with the most pictures is the victor.

Form English Clubs. The clubs can have for their purpose the encouragement of English speech at all times. This is one means of helping the children remember to use English on the school grounds. In one club. eligibility for membership depended upon this very point. If a Mexican child were heard using only English for a certain period of time, he was elected to be a member. If he forgot the rule later, he suffered under a demerit system, and was made to feel the disapproval of his friends.

Provide for many life-situations. If the Mexican child is to learn to use English in real life-situations, he must be given some practice along those lines. The teacher must try to set up problems whose solutions are found through contacts outside the school. It may be possible to send a group of children to an American store in the neighborhood where they must ask questions in English in order to gather data for an arithmetic lesson. Perhaps there is a library nearby where the children are encouraged to go and seek advice from the librarian on the selection of books. Even errands to other rooms in the school are helpful in giving the children needed practice in employing their new language, English.

FOOTNOTES

[1]Nona Rodee, <u>Teaching Beginners to Speak English.</u> (Tucson, Arizona: Tucson Public Schools, 1923), p. 94.

[2]C. C. Crawford and E. M. Leitzell, <u>Learning a New Language</u> (Los Angeles: C. C. Crawford, University of Southern California, 1930), p. 15.

[3]Annie Reynolds, <u>The Education of Spanish-Speaking Children in Five Southwestern States</u> (Bulletin No. 11, United States Government Printing Office). United States Department of the Interior, Office of Education, 1933, p. 14.

[4]Rodee, op. cit., p. 104.

CHAPTER IV

HOW TO TEACH THE READING OF ENGLISH

In the modern educational world, reading, as a school subject, has gained a position of paramount importance. Instead of being classed as just one of the "three 'R's," it is taking its place as THE "R", the keystone, upon which success in other subjects depends. The recognition of this rightful place for reading has grown out of studies and experiments in schools with children who speak a common language. Even in such schools, it is not always easy to teach children to read.

Reading must be thought of as more than just skill in mechanical word-calling, however smoothly that is done. Its broad, functional scope includes many types of reading for varied purposes.

The teachers of Mexican children have before them the enormous task of teaching reading in a language which is foreign to the children and which, unfortunately, remains foreign in far too many cases in spite of the American schools' best efforts.

In teaching Mexican children to read, using the term in its broadest sense, the teacher has a three-fold task before her. Her first step is to build up meanings and ideas in terms of the English language. Next, she must place special emphasis on certain phases of the mechanics of reading. The third very important step in teaching Mexican children to read English is to help them to read with such facility, and to stimulate their enjoyment in reading English to such an extent, that the acquired art will not fall into disuse as soon as the stimuli of school situations and teacher-created enthusiasm and motivation are removed.

Ways of meeting these three major problems in teaching the reading of English to Mexican children are suggested below.

I. BUILD UP MEANINGS

The average American child, at the time he enters school, has had thousands of experiences and has formed ideas from them in terms of the English language. The average Mexican child with whom this study is concerned, has had far fewer, far more limited experiences, and has formed ideas from them in terms of his native tongue.

It is the task of the teacher to build in these Mexican children's minds word meanings and thoughts in English, and then to have them not only pronounce but comprehend and interpre these meanings and thoughts from their written or printed English symbols. Even the simplest words that have been a part of the American child's knowledge from his first moment of language comprehension, must be taught to the Mexican child.

As has been presented in the preceding chapter, the Mexican child is given a limited working command of spoken English in his first few weeks or months of school. He is made familiar with his immediate environment in terms of English speech and thought. Reading must not be attempted until this skill is an inseparable part of the child.

Below are some suggested means by which the teacher may proceed from this limited foundation of spoken English.

<u>Introduce reading vocabulary with conversation.</u> Reading lessons should grow out of definitely planned conversations in which the teacher employs and extracts from the children those words and thoughts which are to appear in the lessons. Speaking is the psychological basis for reading, and the teacher of Mexican children who follows this conversation technique will meet with far greater success than she will if she allows the children, even in the upper grades, to flounder without aid in a sea of unfamiliar words and sentence forms. This point cannot be stressed too strongly. The teacher must remember that a sentence which, even though of inverted or complex form, would be clear in meaning to an American child, would completely confuse the Mexican child whose thoughts and comprehension have of necessity been built on simple, definite, thought and speech patterns.

Use only familiar material at first. Before reading is introduced, the Mexican child should command a working vocabulary of English concerning his own personal self, and his immediate environment of school and home, toys and pets. Out of these should grow his first reading lessons. No attempt is made to add new words to his English vocabulary through reading lessons at first. Instead, the reading and speaking only work together to fasten more firmly in the Mexican child's mind his acquired language ability.

Use pictures and objects. No teacher of American children would attempt to work without a goodly supply of pictures and objects. Certainly no teacher of Mexican children could conduct even a first lesson without these indispensable teaching aids. Since it is advocated that English be taught entirely by the direct method; that is without any Spanish used to convey meanings, pictures and objects serve to bridge the gap of translation. They link in the child's mind the known and the unknown and make them one. For example, the concept of "Mother" is ready-formed in the Mexican child's mind, but in terms of Spanish thought and speech. Many pictures of mothers performing familiar acts such as bathing baby, cooking dinner, or washing clothes, together with accompanying sentences or words will help the Mexican child to comprehend the thoughts and words, and to form his concept in terms of English without the intervening step of conscious translation from Spanish word to English word.

Introduce vocabulary through activities. This is one of the surest ways of supplying varied experiences and comprehended vocabulary. Here the "learn by doing" principle is utilized. Out of activities will come many thoughts that must be guided by the teacher into English channels. These in turn will be written for reading or will be found in a prepared lesson. The Mexican children must not be given time to think of their activities in their vernacular but must be supplied with the English thoughts and new words in as many varying situations as are possible. In this way the task of reading becomes one of word recognition, only, not complicated by a struggle for understanding as well.

Have much dramatization. Dramatizing reading material will give to the

Mexican child a more firm hold on the thoughts he has extracted from the printed page. Too often the teacher is lulled into believing that a group of Mexican children have "got the thought" because they seem to read with such facility, only to be rudely awakened when she asks for a demonstration in dramatized form. Dramatization will clarify muddled thoughts and make them a functioning part of the child.

Use the principle of multiple association. This technique will help the Mexican child to separate words from their initial associations and to broaden his concept of their meanings. To use one example; to the American child, "red" is a color and he can use the word to describe any number of things. To the Mexican child, "red" is a vague word that he has seen and heard in connection with another word, such as "ball." Perhaps the teacher has also used "little" and "rubber" at other times with ball so in order to clarify "red," the teacher must make as many different associations with other words as possible. Colored pictures with the words printed beneath -- "red wagon," "red dress," or "red bird" -- are one illustration of the principle of multiple association.

Teach opposites, present and past of verbs, and singular and plural of nouns. These three groups of word forms are excellent means of adding words and meanings to the Mexican child's vocabulary and knowledge of English. In a city system known to the writer, where a large percentage of the elementary children is Mexican, one, two, or three of the above groups are a part of almost every reading lesson. One way of teaching these groups follows. "T" crosses are drawn and the horizontal lines are appropriately labeled. The children choose words from the lesson to place in the various columns, then fill the blanks with the needed forms. This teaches the Mexican child to read and understand varied word forms.

Teach only basic words in lessons. This is a word of warning to the teacher of limited experience with Mexican children. Most reading material that the teacher must use has been prepared for American children and often words and phrases are used which are clear to those familiar with English but which are beyond the Mexican child's limited comprehension. Unless the words and phrases are basic ones that are needed to understand the story or ones that will be met frequently in the reading lessons, it is better to pass over them lightly and place the emphasis on the basic words and phrases. In her desire to have her charges know what they are reading, the inexperienced teacher of foreign-tongued children is apt to confuse their minds with words that were inserted to relieve the monotony of the story but that are of no value or use to the Mexican child.

Train in extracting meanings from context. This training is a very necessary part of teaching Mexican children to understand what they read. In the lower elementary grades, the language handicap will limit the vocabulary of the reading material for these children, and the teacher can definitely teach the meanings of the words in the lesson. However, as the child advances, he is encouraged to read as widely as he possibly can. He must be taught to study unknown words in their relation to other words in the sentence to find a key to their meaning. This does not mean he should be allowed merely to guess at word meanings and pass on without finding a real basis for his guess in the context. Of course, dictionary work in the upper elementary grades will supplement this work but should not altogether supplant it, as the Mexican, in his later readings, will meet far more unknown words than he could or would seek meanings for in a dictionary.

II. DEVELOP THE MECHANICS OF READING

Anyone who has attempted to pronounce foreign words, no doubt recalls the difficulty he had in making them flow smoothly from his lips. And to recognize printed words and coordinate eye movement with this flow was indeed a task! Yet the little Mexican children with a background of six or seven years of Spanish plus four to eight or nine months of school English are asked to make that blend of skills successfully in order to advance in their school work. To bring this about, the teacher must use every technique at her command; and, in addition, should place special emphasis upon certain phases of the teaching.

In some school systems, special courses of study for teaching the Mexican children in the lower grades have been developed, and readers especially prepared to follow the speech and vocabulary development are available. This facilitates the all-important basic work. However, since many teachers cannot make use of these aids, experienced teachers of Mexican children have offered the suggestions that follow.

Use thoroughly familiar subject matter for early lessons. As the Mexican child's first speaking lesson probably was, "My name is Juan," or some such personal thought vitally interesting to him, so should his first reading be. Not only must the word meanings be clear to him, but he must possess the ability to say the particular word combinations with ease or he will develop a stumbling, halting habit and a jerky eye-movement.

In the upper elementary grades, the pronunciation of difficult words and word combinations in the reading material must be analyzed and drilled on before the child attempts to read them.

Teach complete thoughts first. The teacher of Mexican children must remember that while the ability to recognize printed words is important, the Mexican child must be taught those words in complete thought forms first. If he is to read, write, and speak English thoughts, he must be taught thoughts before isolated words. After the thought is firmly established in his mind, it may be broken down into phrases, words, and letters for word recognition and sounds.

Stress initial sounds, blends, and phonograms. Of course this work is done with all children learning to read, but it is especially important with Mexican children and should be continued with them far longer than with American children. The teacher should use a few minutes of each reading lesson to call the children's attention to certain initial sounds, blends, or phonograms that recur in the lesson and to drill briefly on them. This will clarify the recognition and pronunciation of words and will furnish the necessary keys to new words.

Allow no sub-vocalization. It seems that the Mexican child must receive the words through the ear as well as through the eye when he is supposed to be reading silently. Consequently, the so-called silent reading period in a great many Mexican classes visited by the writer sounded like the buzzing of angry bees as each child read aloud to himself.

This is an easily understood fault, but the teacher must make every effort to overcome the buzzing, the lip movement, and the throat movement. Rapid flash card phrase and sentence drills that are not to be read aloud but that are to be dramatized will help to spead up reading and leave no time for sub-vocalization.

Another suggested remedy is to have the child hold the tip of his tongue in his front teeth, or consciously hold his lips closed until the old desire is overcome.

Watch the child's mouth when he reads. In this way the teacher can detect many errors of pronunciation and enunciation that her ear would miss. The Mexican child must be taught to imitate with his own organs the teacher's placement of her vocal organs, and must be drilled in their proper use lest his speech and reading become a confusion of "t" and "d", "b" and "v", "i" and "e" sounds.

Emphasize word endings. The Mexican child is not conscious of the shades of meanings signified by various word endings. The stem word conveys an idea to him and he is satisfied that he recognizes something familiar so he goes no farther. The teacher must constantly call his attention to endings and drill on meanings conveyed by them. A simple and pleasing little device for getting the children to notice and sound the endings is to have them count the "puppies" who want to wag their tails, then have the children "wag the puppies' tails" when they read the sentence.

Give ear training. It is often very helpful to the Mexican children to have the teacher read a lesson to them, emphasizing the proper phrasing and expression, then to have them imitate her. This will aid them in developing a feeling for phrasing and for English inflections.

One upper grade teacher used an amusing device for this ear training. She had a stack of drill cards with sentences of ambiguous meanings on them. These were to be read and interpreted according to the phrasing used. Two examples are "John said Mary will do it now," and "The little boy said his mother jumped over the fence." The teacher or a child would read the sentence, phrasing it to bring out one of the meanings he desired, then would ask for an explanation. If the child called upon had properly sensed the meaning conveyed and could explain it, he was awarded a point in the reading game.

Avoid concert reading. Teachers to whom the writer has talked express the opinion that with Mexican children, concert reading and speaking give too greatly an opportunity for the formation of slovenly or incorrect pronunciation and enunciation habits. Therefore, any advantages this technique may have with American children are overshadowed by these dangers for Mexican children.

Stimulate clear enunciation. Because most of the Mexican children have little opportunity to associate with English-speaking people who enunciate precisely, their ears are not trained to clear-cut sounds in English words. Hence, the teacher must do all in her power to make up this deficiency. She must be sound-conscious and insist that words be clearly said. A good groundwork of phonics and vocal organ exercises will help to develop the child's ability in enunciation.

Reading to an audience, especially to one with less knowledge of English than he has, will encourage the Mexican child to be careful and precise with his sounds.

Another powerful stimulus is the criticism of his classmates, whose approval he is of course eager to win.

Review constantly. Any teacher knows how discouraging the results of a test over supposedly familiar material often are, and they are not always complicated by a language handicap. Let the teacher of Mexican children take heed and review constantly. Where the American child would be utterly bored with reading the same story again and again, the Mexican child needs and actually enjoys this many-fold repetition. He gains much ability to read and interpret because the material is familiar, and he also gains the much-needed self-confidence that comes with treading upon known ground. Let the Mexican do much of this very helpful type of reading.

III. STIMULATE THE DESIRE TO READ ENGLISH MATERIAL

The teacher of Mexican children must always keep in mind the wide difference in background between American children and Mexicans. Hardly an American home exists that does not possess books, magazines, or newspapers; and on every hand there are labels, signs, and directions to be read. Reading becomes second nature;

a matter of course. In the Mexican home, from whence come the class of children to which the writer has reference in this study, there is a dearth of printed material, even in Spanish, and a noticeable lack of ability to read in either Spanish or English.

Therefore, the teacher must endeavor to fix most firmly in her Mexican children the reading habit. They must find the reading of English so pleasurable that the great effort required to do it will be overlooked or overcome. Suggested ways of establishing this reading habit follow.

Surround the child with interesting, illustrated material. Pictures of all kinds with short sentences and stories below are one sure means of encouraging Mexican children to read. The illustrations help the child to understand the accompanying words.

Have the children make booklets of their own drawings with explanations below and place these on the class library table. The pictures can be scenes from their own personal experiences, or can be illustrations of parts of their reading lessons with the appropriate sentences copied below.

Supply plenty of familiar reading matter. Here again the child-made booklets function. For example, a class studying a unit on airplanes or sports gathers pictures for a scrapbook. A series of stories are written by the class and pasted below the pictures. The book is then used for reading review over familiar material. The Mexican children never seem to tire of going over the stories again and again.

They also enjoy reading for themselves a story that has been read aloud and explained to them by the teacher. They feel familiar with the content and the difficult words can be read with ease.

Emphasize content and story rather than skill in reading mechanics at times. Even though so much time must necessarily be spent on reading mechanics with Mexican children, the teacher must give a great deal of time to the pure enjoyment of reading, too, if her Mexican children are to develop a love for it. She will often have to search diligently through many books for stories that are at the proper interest level and yet are in language simple enough for comprehension. She should devote time each day to the pleasure-type of reading in which she stresses the thoughts conveyed and minimizes her corrections and drills on mechanics.

Use written directions in many forms. The more children read, the easier it becomes for them to do so. Written directions, as well as oral ones, in which the children are forced to interpret precisely are another means of establishing the reading habit. Much interesting seat work and many games can be devised in which worthwhile reading abilities are developed.

Provide material of surprise content. Letters and stories written by the children and exchanged with each other or with another class always find eager readers. Another device is a game in which pictures illustrating parts of a simple story are passed out and the children must find the sentences which describe the picture and read them. In these and many other ways, the Mexican children learn that the reading of English is a pleasure.

Organize reading clubs. Such organizations are so necessary to give the Mexican children confidence in themselves. They gain a great deal of self-assurance in their ability to handle the English language when they are able to hold places in reading clubs, especially if Americans are also members. The wise teacher will promote many such clubs with her Mexican pupils.

Make available reading matter on hobbies and special interest. The powerful stimuli of hobbies and special interests will carry Mexican boys and girls through very difficult English reading matter. In such reading, the same vocabulary is met frequently in many different constructions. It becomes a fixed part of the child and gives him assurance in its use because the varied associations have amplified the concepts in his mind.

The teacher who encourages such reading in her Mexican children gives them an invaluable gift--a worthwhile leisure-time activity which is sure to hold within them the ability and the desire to read English.

Develop an interest in periodicals. This can be done in various ways. "My Weekly Reader" and "My Weekly Primer" are two excellent and reasonable little papers designed for schoolroom use.

The teacher can develop a unit on a sport, such as baseball, and have the daily papers closely followed for news. She will doubtless find that though the homes are unsupplied with papers, the children will make great effort to seek out and bring in the news each day.

Continued stories in children's magazines and the so-called comics in the newspapers are two other means of developing the Mexican children's interest in the reading of English periodicals.

This work can be extended into the home if the teacher can gather magazines from her friends and send them home by the children. Magazines are usually a rare treat in the Mexican home and they are highly treasured.

Cultivate the library habit. Mexicans are timid and very often do without what they want rather than approach Americans and ask for it. Therefore, it is important that the teacher acquaint her Mexican pupils with all of the mysteries of library procedures--be the library a classroom one, a central school one, or a public one in the community.

There are many lures with which she can bait their interests until the library habit is firmly established. She can take them on instructional visits; she can send some to obtain books for her; she can establish a small library within her room if her book supply permits, and have the children officiate. There are a hundred other ways to bring about her objectives: to make her Mexican pupils book-conscious; to overcome their awe of the unknown; and to make them eager to seek knowledge and entertainment in the land of English reading.

CHAPTER V

HOW TO COMBAT THE COMMON CONDITION OF POOR HEALTH

Those people who live in states where great numbers of Mexicans abound and know the deplorable conditions under which they live, realize the extreme importance of health education in the schools. Even though Mexican and American alike are surrounded by health advertisements and instruction, the Mexican has no background for comprehension. He does not know the language so he does not understand the spoken word or the printed matter. He has no money with which to seek medical aid. In his ignorance, tinged with superstition, he has been preyed upon by "quacks" who have brought him harm and fear. This fear, coupled with the fear that attends the unknown, have made him shun aid and overlook advice which might have bettered his conditions.

From the American point of view, the race as a whole is known for its lack of cleanliness and observance of other health habits, its diseases, and its limited diet of highly seasoned foods. Science has proved that all these are directly opposed to the acquisition and preservation of health; and with it, mental welfare; a properly developed personality; and a wholesome social adjustment.

It, then, becomes the duty of the teachers of Mexican children to place stress upon health instruction so that conditions among the Mexicans in the United States will be greatly improved.

They can do this in two ways. They can develop within the individuals a knowledge of personal health habits and a desire to pursue these habits; and they can encourage these individuals to put into practice in their homes the knowledge they acquire in the schoolroom. The teachers must remember that they will not be able to change racial customs and beliefs overnight, but over a period of time a decided change for the better will be noticeable in the health conditions of the

Mexican school children.

I. DEVELOP IDEAS OF PERSONAL HEALTH

Health to the Mexican is something either he has or he does not have. He has a pitiful lack of knowledge of proper health habits, such as eating nourishing, well-balanced diets, taking adequate, regular rest under favorable conditions, and keeping his person clean in order to prevent vermin and disease.

These are the topics which the teachers of Mexican children must stress in their schoolrooms. They must attempt to establish firmly enough in the children the proper health habits so that the ignorance and the indolent attitude in the homes will be somewhat overcome.

The very keynote of all this health instruction must be positive--the desirability of good health rather than the dangers of ill health--lest the children be filled with more fears and apprehensions than they already possess when health and its attendant connotations of doctors and medicine are mentioned.

Ways in which the teacher can establish these personal health ideas in the Mexican childrens' minds follow.

Discuss personal cleanliness. This is a subject which teachers of American children, except possibly those in slum areas, would hesitate to approach too vigorously. However, teachers of Mexican children must cover the topic in all its phases as these children rarely possess any knowledge of its necessity when they come to school.

Some of the little children are pathetic sights--hair long, matted, dirty, and infested with lice; skin broken out in sores and covered with a coating of dirt which is days old; clothing stiff with filth. These conditions exist in city, as well as country, schools.

The teacher is faced with the delicate task of insisting that her children clean up, and doing it tactfully enough so that the parents will cooperate.

In her discussions of personal cleanliness, she can explain very simply some of the body functions and give reasons why people should be clean if the children are advanced enough to comprehend. She can have one or two demonstrate the brushing of teeth and can emphasize its necessity and the clean feeling of the mouth. She can show through pantomine how the father can cut the hair and the mother or child can wash it. (She will not always be successful in getting the girls' hair cut as Mexicans favor long hair for the girls.) She can explain why the skin develops sores if it is not clean. She can praise those who are clean and hold them up as examples for the others to emulate.

In all of these discussions she must take care not to make the poor little unfortunates, whose home conditions defy every effort at betterment, feel that they are not welcome because they are not clean.

Have daily health inspections. These will teach the children several good habits. They will make a daily effort to be clean and neat and they will be shown the necessity of immediate care for an injury or an illness.

If the school does not have a clinic, the teacher should provide herself with a few simple remedies and bandages. Such care as she can give the children daily will do much toward overcoming the fear of treatment that the Mexicans seem to possess. This fear grows out of the fact that through ignorance, the sick are neglected until the situation becomes acute. A doctor is then summoned, or the patient is removed to a hospital where it is often too late to aid him and he dies. Of course this develops a dread of doctors, medicine, and hospitals that must be broken down in the children.

The teacher can use health charts for daily checking or starring and the children feel great pride in watching their own records improve. Charts sent home for marking are not a good idea because the temptation to win approval often causes the children to mark them unfairly.

The children themselves like to be the inspectors, and often the appointment of a particularly dirty child to the position will inspire him to make himself clean.

Provide means for cleaning up. Some schools have well-equipped shower rooms or lavatories; but in others, these are entirely missing. If the teacher expects her children to develop habits of cleanliness, she must make provision for carrying out her teaching. She can see that clean water in a barrel, bucket, or basin is provided if there is no running water in her school. She can take advantage of offers of soap, toothbrush, or toothpaste companies for free samples and reduced rates. She can provide rags if not towels for drying. She can supervise the clean up, or have the children in the upper grades appointed as monitors to oversee the washing of the little ones.

Teach sanitation. It is a common practice among Mexicans to use family combs, toothbrushes, cups, and other property. Reasons why this practice is harmful must be impressed upon the childrens' minds. They must be shown how to drink from a fountain without touching its rim. Monitors should be placed near the fountain to see that the proper habits are developed in the drinking process.

The teacher can discourage the practice of borrowing and lending personal property in the schoolroom, giving reasons that the children can understand.

The children must be given definite instruction in the necessity of clean rest room habits because facilities for indoor sanitation are not common in Mexican homes.

The teacher, or the children themselves if they are old enough, can take advantage of the many offers in advertisements for booklets, charts, and other such material that stress sanitation, often in very cleverly worked-out units or projects.

Develop units on health. Health need not be taught as health alone. It can be coupled with other material in units and be made doubly interesting. For instance, a study of milk, from the careful feeding of the cow, through the stages of sanitary handling, to the care and consumption of the milk in the home is one means of teaching some aspects of health. Other food products could be made to lend themselves readily to such a unit plan also.

Another health unit which the writer used was based upon baseball and the players. Training and health rules governing a Big League team holding spring training in a southern city were discovered and used as models for class training and health rules for the teams in the grade. One phase of this work particularly enjoyed was the collecting of magazine pictures illustrating the rules, and the construction of colorful posters with health rules in cut-out letters. These were used to illustrate little baseball and health talks in other rooms of the school.

Make provision for proper food at school if possible. Mexican people eat a very limited diet which consists chiefly of meat, beans, rice, and corn, all highly seasoned. Their taste for such foods as milk and vegetables must be cultivated.

The way one school encouraged the consumption of vegetables was to plant a school garden and use the produce to prepare soup for the children. This work, from the gardening to the serving of the soup was done entirely by the children, who incidentally received invaluable experience in the proper preparation of foods.

Another school provided nourishing foods at little cost by purchasing from a big market good but slightly wilted or old vegetables which were about to be discarded because the better trade would not buy them. The sum used for buying was made up of small monthly donations of teachers and principal. The soup, containing a quantity of the vegetables, was sold for a penny or two a cup to replenish in part the working capital.

In one place a friendly baker willingly donated stale bread which was soaked in the soup and eaten.

Some communities have organizations which adopt a group of under privileged children and provide for their needs. The teacher might be able to contact such an organization to furnish her little undernourished Mexicans with milk for a mid-morning lunch. Parent-Teacher groups also do much of this worthy work.

If the school is of mixed enrollment or if it embraces several levels of society, those children who can afford it might be encouraged to bring extra lunch to be left in a central place and divided among the needy.

These are only a few of the plans that have been adopted and carried out successfuly to provide proper food for the undernourished Mexican children. However, no matter what means is used, the teacher must always teach the value of the foods and must prove this value through weight and growth charts which will substantiate her claims in concrete form.

Have daily rest periods. A national custom of several countries, Mexico included, is the "siesta," or mid-day rest period. This is one custom the teacher will do well to encourage with her Mexican children. In connection with this rest time, she can teach many conditions that are necessary for proper relaxation and sleep.

Mexican homes are usually very crowded, and several persons either sleep in a bed at once or take turns in using it. The beds are dirty. The value of fresh air is unknown, as is the value of regular, sufficient hours of sleep.

In the upper grades, unless special provisions are made for cots and separate rooms for the boys and girls, the rest plans might be limited to quiet reading in a comfortable, airy room or in the shade of a tree outside.

With the smaller children, each could have a little rug upon which to lie on the floor for a brief nap. However, in either case, instruction in clean, loose clothing, clean beds, proper ventilation, and need for long hours of restful sleep could be given.

Encourage the wearing of clean clothes. Because of their poor economic condition, many Mexican children do not possess more than one dress or pair of trousers and shirt at a time. It is quite a problem to get them to keep these clothes in any condition even approaching cleanliness.

The teacher can suggest every two or three days that the clothes be washed. She can stress the fact that they need not be ironed if they are smoothed out while drying. She can comment on those each day whose clothes look clean. She can try to make some provision for supplying an extra change, then insist that the child wash his own clothes if necessary in order to wear clean ones. If conditions permit, she might even make provisions for boys and girls to wash and dry their clothes under her supervision. In these and other ways she could develop in their minds the idea of clean clothing as one more requisite of personal health.

Provide for proper exercise through organized games. Mexicans, by nature, are not very active people. This is partly due to temperament, and partly due to undernourishment and lack of vitality. Their ability to drowse lazily in the sun for hours is well-known. If the teacher wishes to overcome this tendency in her children and build in them vigorous health, she must teach them proper exercise in such a way that it will be carried on even beyond her encouragement and influence. This will call for organized games, such as baseball; the idea being that the urging of some will cause many to participate in the games and exercises for recreational pasttime outside school hours. Thus does the teacher provide one more way for the development of personal health in her Mexican children.

II. ENCOURAGE HIGHER HEALTH STANDARDS IN THE HOMES

No matter to what lengths the teacher may go to instruct her Mexican children in personal health, she will meet with very limited success unless she can also teach them ways of raising the health standards in their homes.

Many of these children come from shacks of one or two rooms in which families of six, eight, ten, or more persons exist. The yard is probably covered with trash and becomes a mud-hole during rainy weather. Very likely the windows have never known screening and the panes are broken out. Within the house there is a confusion of broken furniture, dirty beds (possibly containing a sick person), and the annual babies. Many of these shacks are adobe huts with dirt floors.

Of course, a great many Mexicans live under conditions far superior to those described, but a trip through the Mexican areas in the United States near the border of Mexico would show that the description is hardly exaggerated.

It is the teacher's job to find out the existing conditions and help the children, and through them the parents, to better these conditions in order to bring about more healthful living.

Ways in which teachers might help their Mexican children to bring about this betterment follow.

Discuss home conditions. The tactful teacher can, through little stories and indirect questions, lead her children to reveal unsatisfactory conditions under which they live. She will probably learn that flies and mosquitoes swarm through the hut day and night; that food is not protected in any way; that the sick sleep and live with the well, no matter what the disease; that there is no bathroom or indoor plumbing of any kind; and that the yards and surrounding grounds are covered with trash and stagnant pools. When these or other similar conditions are found to be common to the group, the teacher must begin her work to bring about a gradual improvement.

Suggest ways to improve certain conditions. Many Mexicans are willing and even able to improve conditions if they are but shown the necessity and told how it can be done. A sand table model of a typical Mexican home is a very interesting and effective way of showing how certain conditions can be improved. After lessons on the harmful effects of flies and mosquitoes, the children could screen the windows and put in a little system of drainage ditches to clear stagnant pools. In connection with this, a lesson on the purification of water by boiling could be given. Such points of sanitation as the advantageous placement of outhouses and wells can also be illustrated on the sand table.

Studies of "Popular Mechanics" or other similar publications are another way of offering suggestions for improvement in the homes.

A study of many pictures of simple, attractive homes might set up within the children a distinct feeling of dissatisfaction with their own abodes and out of this dissatisfaction will come changes.

Give instruction on food sanitation. This can be done through a grocery store unit. As part of the work, it may be possible to take the class on a visit to some modern store where devices for food protection are studied. Reasons for the care of food may be studied and ways worked out that will be possible in a home devoid of ice and screens.

Teach home nursing. Sickness is very common among the Mexicans, and the mortality rate is often appalling, especially among infants. These conditions are due in part to the utter ignorance of these people. They seem to know nothing of the necessity of isolation for one who is ill, or of the proper handling of him and the things used in his illness. They are a morbidly curious people who flock in during illness or death, regardless of the cause or of the consequence to themselves. Quarantine rules mean nothing to them.

Hence, the teacher must instill into the minds of her children some of the simple rules of home nursing. She can seize opportunities of injury or illness among the children themselves to illustrate her points; or she can set up a little sick room corner with dolls as patients. The children can learn much practical knowledge by playing "doctor and nurse."

Provide simple remedies. The simple remedies, such as hot salt water, hot and cold packs, soda, soothing salves, oil of cloves, and iodine, that have brought relief in many American households seem to be unknown in the Mexican home. Even good warm soapy water, which is a fine preventative in many cases, is not always to be had.

When a teacher sends a sick or injured child home, she should try to send some healing remedy and specific directions with him. Hot salt water for an eye swollen almost shut by a sty, or for an inflamed throat have done much to relieve suffering that would have gone unnoticed or unaided but for the teacher. A bar of soap and some healing salve, furnished by the teacher, will often help some child to rid himself of scabies, or "the itch," a trouble so common among the Mexicans.

"La maestra" is held in reverence by many Mexicans, and her directions are carried out as a priest's would be. Because of this feeling, she can do much from her schoolroom post to better the Mexican's health conditions.

Insist upon neatness of school desk, room, and yard. The children can be taught that their school is their second home and that they are responsible for its appearance. The teacher must show them how to care for this property; how to arrange the rooms attractively with pictures and flowers; how to keep the floors free of paper and mud; how to dispose of lunch papers so that the yards will not be littered. If conditions permit, the children can be directed in real clean-up tasks, such as washing woodwork and windows, cleaning floors, trimming grass, and burning trash.

At all times the teacher must make the children conscious of the similarity between the work they do at school and the work they can do in their own homes to improve the living conditions there.

Study various types of home. One way to do this is to develop some such topic as, "Homes Around the World," emphasizing in the study the way in which different types of homes are kept clean and attractive. Another way is through the beautiful advertisements that fill most magazines.

The teacher's great task is to make her children conscious enough of beauty and cleanliness that they will want to change their own conditions in order to get them.

Have dramatizations of home situations. Two particularly bad conditions that exist among many Mexicans are their eating and their sleeping habits.

The Mexican family is truly a patriarchal one. The father usually sits to eat and is served by other members of the family. The children rarely compose themselves for a decent meal, but snatch a bite somewhere while running around or doubled up in some corner. The teacher must try to develop more correct eating habits in her children. One way to do this is through little tea parties, real or imaginary. Another way is through the mid-morning lunch or noon lunch period. Simple table manners, pleasant conversation, and the careful mastication of food can be stressed at these times. These practices must be continued frequently if they are to become habitual.

As for sleeping habits, the teacher can have many little playlets in which dolls are made ready for bed at a certain time each day, placed carefully in clean beds, and windows are adjusted for proper ventilation. She can stress the importance of rest for children, of loose clothing, and of sleeping alone. However, she can only hope that such instructions will carry over into homes where usually far too many people occupy far too little floor space and depend upon all the clothing they own and their proximity to another body to take the place of covering for warmth.

Teach privacy. Because of crowded conditions, such a thing as privacy in the Mexican home is practically unknown. These very conditions will balk many of the teacher's efforts, but she must attempt to teach her children the value of privacy at times, as it will make for more wholesome emotional control.

She must urge that the children try to find places to sleep alone, that they perform certain acts out of the sight of others, and that they observe the rights of others at all times. Perhaps the best way to bring about the desired end is by having little instructional talks with the children and by giving to each certain properties and positions not to be trespassed upon by the others.

Thus, in the ways mentioned and in many others the teachers can strive to improve the personal and home health conditions of their Mexican charges.

CHAPTER VI

HOW TO DEAL WITH RACIAL TRAITS

No doubt many a beginning teacher, faced with a classroom full of little Mexican children, has felt as though she were transplanted in a foreign land. These children, true to their heritage, display many racial traits that seem quite different from American characteristics.

Racial traits draw upon many sources for their being. Centuries have gone into the building up of the folkways and mores of a people. The laws, customs, education, economic status, and religious beliefs all are contributors to the characteristics displayed by a race, and the source of an individual one cannot be traced.

Indeed, it cannot be said even that all members of that race will display its traits. Science today recognizes too strongly that individual differences make it impossible to point to a "typical" Mexican or a "typical" American and say that his actions are an example of the characteristics of his race.

However, many students of the subject, experienced teachers, and social workers among Mexicans have, after spending considerable time with these people, been able to plot certain trends of thinking and action. It is so necessary for the teacher, particularly if she is an inexperienced one, to learn something about these trends, so that she can strengthen and develop the desirable ones, and overcome or guide into more worthy paths those thought by Americans to be less desirable.

I. DEVELOP THE DESIRABLE TRAITS

It is a deplorable fact that far too many Americans, particularly those of the Southwest who use the Mexicans for what labor they can get out of them then fling them aside as so much dry pulp, fail to see and to utilize for the betterment of everyone concerned the many desirable characteristics these Mexicans display.

Fortunately, all teachers worthy of the title are conscious of the value of character and personality traits and of the necessity of utilizing them in the development of the wholesome personality.

The teacher's surest approach to these Mexican children is through sincerity and kindness--rarities in their lives among Americans. Her strongest ally is the Mexicans' sensitiveness to praise or blame. She must make them conscious of their worth by pointing out and praising all the good traits, whether racial or individual, so that these traits may be strengthened. At all times the teacher must make the children conscious that these desirable traits exist within them, and that by exercising them, the children may gain the respect and friendship of those with whom they associate.

Ways to develop some of the most noticeable racial traits are suggested below.

Cultivate the love of color and beauty. This admiration for color and beauty is plainly shown in many ways: by the vivid colors selected whenever a choice is possible; by the beautiful patterns of colorful handwork that adorn the Mexicans' clothing, particularly their native dress; by the vivid "serapes" of the "caballeros;" and by the bright flowers that may be seen blooming in almost every Mexican home, no matter how lowly.

The teacher can stimulate this love of color and beauty by turning her classroom into an attractive workshop and display room. She can secure magazines filled with bright advertisements and study with her class the skillful blending of colors displayed in them. She can secure from paint distributors and manufacturers color cards and pamphlets of suggestions on color combinations.

She can encourage the children to do much work in which color plays an important part; making posters, drawing with crayolas, painting, and construction work with colored paper.

One teacher, a student of art herself, procured excellent colored prints of the world's masterpieces and studied with her classes the artists' use of their colors for various effects. Another teacher devoted some time to the study of combining colored fabrics. A third, who had a beautiful view of field and lake from her window, constantly called the children's attention to the shifting scenes of beauty in nature. In some classrooms visited there were found window boxes and pots of bright flowers. In one grade, a school flower garden project was found to be in progress.

Such activities as these described suggest to the Mexican children many ways to satisfy their love of beauty and to brighten the drab, ugly surroundings most of them are forced to live in.

Encourage generosity. This admirable trait of generosity is very noticeable among the Mexican people. The children willingly share with one another their meagre possessions. Wallace Thompson says,

> One of the most noticeable traits shown by Mexican children is the spirit of charity shown toward anyone, especially toward persons of their own race. As a rule the Mexican possesses but little of worldly goods, but the little they have they will always share with those in distress. Natural beggars themselves, they never turn a deaf ear to the needy.[1]

The Mexican families readily take in unfortunate relatives or friends who are in need of help and give of what they have. In fact, it is the custom to accord the newcomers all rights and privileges of members of the family, and they are expected to feel that they are as much a part of the group as though they were born into it.

The teacher must praise this generosity. She must understand that it will be practiced on her and that she must accept, in the spirit in which they are offered, the little treasures these children bring her— gaily-dyed feather, a pretty smooth agate marble, a piece of candy (no doubt saved from some very special treat), a beautiful little picture of some religious figure, or a bow of ribbon. She can show the children that she values these gifts and make them feel joy in giving.

The teacher herself in turn can give the children little scraps of bright paper, ribbons, or little pictures and encourage them to take part of the gift home to the ever-present little brothers and sisters.

Another way to encourage generosity is to provide opportunities for the children to make little gifts, such as bookmarks or greeting cards for other children in the school. Of course, holidays and special occasions always offer chances to make gifts for others, either in the school or at homes.

One teacher cleverly aimed toward her goal by organizing a Generous Deeds Club. The membership privileges depended upon the acts of real generosity the teacher herself saw among her children in the classroom and on the playground. When she noticed such an act, she would write the name of the child and a little notation of the deed on a small slip of paper and drop it into the box provided for the purpose. On a certain day of each week the box was opened and the names and deeds discussed and praised. The teacher tried to curb any desire on the part of the children to act merely for effect by ignoring such obvious acts and choosing only those which really seemed unstudied and sincere.

Utilize the loyalty and patriotism. This loyalty and patriotism manifests itself in a fierce love of Mexico and all things Mexican, even though many of the children, and possibly their parents, were born within the borders of the United States and have never seen Mexico. However, this feeling is readily understood when one knows that the younger generations are fed upon stories of "the good old days" in a Mexico that is made to seem like a Utopia. It is a country to which they cling for a feeling of security and "belonging" while they live in another nation without having been assimilated to its laws and customs, and among a people who have never accorded them a place of equality in society.

The teacher must try to awaken in her Mexican children a kindred feeling toward America and things American. She can direct this feeling by favorable comparisons of the advantages of the two countries. She can conduct flag ceremonies in which both the American and Mexican flags have parts. She can stir the children's emotional natures with patriotic poems and music. She must try to make the children feel that America is to them what Mexico is to their parents or grandparents who came from there.

In some Mexican communities there exist patriotic organizations, some for the purpose of preserving the allegiance of Mexicans to Mexico, and others which encourage allegiance of the Mexicans to their adopted country, the United States. The teacher may be able to learn of such societies in her community and pattern some children's patriotic clubs after them.

In all dealings with her children, the teacher must hold one thought above others. She must never belittle anything Mexican if she wishes to have success in redirecting their strong feeling of loyalty and patriotism toward America.

Provide for much handwork. Mexicans for centuries have been hand workers. In this kind of work they can feel success and with it, happiness. Many of them possess home-developed skills such as clay-molding, pottery-making, and fine needlework. The teacher can encourage these abilities and many others by introducing units of work that require many construction activities.

In one such unit, a study of the pioneer log cabin, the Mexican children built the cabin, furnished it, dressed clothespin dolls, set up a forest back of the cabin, populated it with Indians and wild animals, then made placards and attractive booklets to explain the work.

Another group, in a transportation unit, constructed many models of early and late vehicles to add to an existent classroom museum.

Since it is quite probable that most of the Mexicans in the United States will have to provide for themselves by the use of their hands, the teacher will do well to utilize this aptitude that they display and develop skill in the use of many kinds of materials and tools.

Supplement natural courtesy with other manners. Mexicans are among the most courteous people in the world. They have what Americans think of as "Old World" manners. They do not understand, particularly the older ones, the curt American "Thanks," the mere nod of greeting, or the lift of a hand and a "So Long" on departure.

The teacher must try to preserve the beautiful customs of courtesy; the bow, the unfailing handshake, the softly murmured "Muchas gracias, senority" or "maestra," and at the same time teach some of the more abrupt, but accepted, American ways if the children are to be made at ease in American society.

The teacher can establish and consistently carry out certain practices in the everyday classroom life, such as always passing behind other persons; having the boys offer chairs to girls and to visitors, pick up fallen articles, carry packages, remove caps on entering a building and on meeting ladies; and by having the children learn to greet and entertain visitors and to address older people with polite English phrases.

Accepted manners elsewhere can be taught through dramatization. Some opportunity for instruction in courtesy can be included in almost every reading lesson which lends itself to dramatization.

Little plays can be written to include experiences which the children need. For example, telephones are rare among the Mexicans with which this writing deals. Yet the children, particularly the older ones who often must quit school to work, need to know the telephone courtesies practiced by some Americans if not by all. Such experiences can be supplied through plays and dramatized stories.

In all her teaching, the teacher must remember that her actions are the examples which will have the greatest influence on the children, so her manners must be the ones she wishes to have reflected by her Mexican pupils.

Satisfy the love of music and dancing. The Mexican people indulge in a great deal of music and dancing for their entertainment. It is their custom to have evening parties in their homes--"tertulias," they are called--and many individuals and groups entertain the guest with such dances as "Baile Tapatilo," "El Jarabe Mexicano," and "La Jota"--hat dances; and "Las Espuelas"--a spur dance, in which the performer beats out a quick rhythm with his jangling spurs. Many of the children, even tiny tots, are encouraged to take part in the gaieties and develop into expert and nimble little dancers at an early age.

Mexican music is usually made on the strings and bands of strolling serenaders can be found in many of the cities and towns near the border strumming their guitars in front of homes where people are gathered outside to enjoy the "symphony under the stars."

The teacher can find many ways to encourage this love of music and rhythm.

In one Mexican school in San Antonio, Texas, there was organized a rhythm band of about thirty little pre-primer and first grade musicians. They were constumed in their native Mexican dress and performed so cleverly that they were in great demand for programs throughout the city.

The teacher can usually find many songs to fit phases of her unit work. For example, songs pertaining to travel, an Indian birch canoe, a bus, a train, and an airplane were included in a unit on transportation in one class visited.

For recreational periods the teacher can teach many little singing and rhythm games and can encourage the Mexican children to display their talents as performers of their own Mexican dances. The writer's own school is situated near a recreation center where free instruction in tap dancing was offered, and many of the children were encouraged to take part in the classes and to display their progress to their classmates in the schoolroom.

Of course, individual and group singing, victrolas, and radios are other possibilities that the teacher can utilize in satisfying the Mexican children's strong love for music.

Praise the love of family. Another national trait worthy of cultivation among the Mexicans is their love of family. The Mexican family is often a large one. It is distinctly patriarchal in organization. The father's word is law. Sons are preferred, though the women and girls are accorded much love and respect and often lead very sheltered lives.

The regard and thoughtfulness of brothers and sisters for one another and their love for the absent ones, older or younger, are very noticeable among the Mexican children at school.

The teacher can foster these admirable feelings by teaching the children how they may better care for the ones at home. She can encourage them to teach the little ones English. She can have some special school exercise and permit the children to bring the little brothers and sisters--something they all love to do-- and by admiring these babies, she can completely win the hearts of her pupils.

In some communities, particularly where there are quite a few Americans in the group with the Mexicans, the teacher might find that the Mexican children do not like to tell how many members there are in the family. Some of them seem to feel shame at the large number of brothers and sisters they have in comparison with the smaller American families. The teacher must do all she can to reduce this feeling by encouraging the children to tell of the achievements of the family members and by praising their love for each other. She can find many stories of family life that will help her in this work.

In the lower grades, the subject matter often lends itself to use with a play family in the room. In this connection the teacher can point out many advantages of large families. Even in the upper grades, much dramatization of family life will furnish the teacher with many opportunities to praise the Mexican's love of family.

II. OVERCOME THE UNDESIRABLE TRAITS

In addition to many admirable traits, Mexican children display several undesirable ones as well. Of course, these are reflections of the habits of a race whose history depicts oppression rather than freedom; ignorance instead of knowledge; and whose climate encourages languor and stagnation rather than industry and advancement.

Those familiar with the Mexican people list such traits as irresponsibility, imitativeness, thriftlessness, sex-consciousness, individualism, and procrastination as being among the ones which hold them on the low plane at which most of them in the United States exist.

The school may not be able to perform miracles and remake a race in a few short months or years, but if the teacher is aware that such characteristics may manifest themselves, she need not wait for the first signs. She can safely choose the antitheses of the above list as her goals and aim toward them. She will be doing her bit toward helping the Mexicans to improve their lot and to find greater favor in the American eye.

Suggested ways of combatting these undesirable traits follow:

Develop a sense of responsibility. Mexicans are prone to shun responsibility and accept authority too readily. They have been forced to submit to leaders too long and the habit is strong upon them.

It is the task of the teacher to make her Mexican children feel the weight of certain responsibilities if she wishes to develop this trait within them. One way to do this is to inaugurate a monitor system and hold each individual accountable for his work every day. In one classroom visited, a bright, colorful monitor chart hung in a prominent place on the wall. Below an attractive picture were slits into which names of monitors for the week could be inserted. It was considered a privilege to have one's name on the chart, and only those who proved themselves worthy of the responsibility were selected and retained.

Another way to make the child feel responsibility is to have much group activity in which each part is very dependent upon other parts for its proper functioning. If one child fails to do his share, he will quickly feel the disapproval of the group, and group disfavor can be a very powerful stimulus in bringing the erring one back into line.

The teacher must shift responsibility to the children at all possible times if she expects to develop this trait within them. For example, choose leaders and make them responsible for the conduct of their groups during auditorium programs of special playground activities. Help the children to plan entertainments, but make them responsible for the successful carrying out of the plans. Refrain from stepping in to save a situation if someone fails to do his part. Allow the children themselves to work out the problem. In this and many other ways, the children will learn to assume responsibilities and carry through projects by themselves.

Promote initiative and self-dependence. Mexicans are necessarily forced to be imitators of Americans, consciously or unconsciously, in their life among them. So much of the school program for the education of the Mexican children is set up upon this very imitative basis. This naturally dulls any originativeness they possess. One means of counterbalancing this is by encouraging much creative work. One way this can be done is by allowing time each day for original drawings illustrating stories read to the children or by them. Mexicans are copyists and the children will want to see the pictures in the book before drawing, but the teacher must help them to develop their imaginations for original rather than copied work.

Another way is by forming a student organizations in which the children must depend upon their own initiative to originate and carry through projects. The leaders in such organizations must be changed often so that the old tendency of the Mexicans to be followers will be overcome and initiative will be developed in many rather than in only a few.

Encourage thrift. The Mexicans seem to have little foresight and rarely feel the necessity of preparing for the future by practicing thrift and economy with the present moment's plenty. Many of them work very hard for a short time and accumulate dollars and possessions, then quit their work to enjoy the fruits of their labors with no thoughts of the time when these things will be gone. They seem not to know how to take care of what they have in order to make it last longer.

To overcome these thriftless tendencies, the teacher must teach many ways to prepare for the rainy days that will come. For example, in one classroom in a district where the children made a good many nickels and dimes by shining shoes and selling newspapers, a wall chart attested to a little banking contest in progress. Another chart explained budget system with percentages for food, clothing, shelter, recreation, and savings listed. At the end of each month the children proudly recounted to an audience of classmates or visitors the results of this thrift venture.

In another room, the children were taught thrift of another kind--that of repairing their clothing in order to make it last longer. A large sewing kit was provided in a corner where a screen could be set up if necessary. As may be expected, the proverb, "A stitch in time saves nine," was prominently displayed and the children were urged to observe its homely truth almost daily.

Another teacher, who encouraged a great deal of work with construction paper, taught thrift by emphasizing the proper placement of pattern on paper in order to save as much as possible. Scraps were preserved and the children were taught to test them first for use before they took a new sheet to cut into. This point was used as the basis for discussions on how many other materials could be conserved.

Overcome sex-consciousness. This overconsciousness of the other sex is probably the result of centuries of chaperonage and separation of the sexes. It is very noticeable; even in the little children. Little Mexican girls will huddle in a group and can scarcely be coaxed to sit closer than a second chair from the little boys.

The teacher must endeavor to promote a more wholesome attitude between them without making them conscious that she is aware of the feeling. She can pair them off in lines, using little brother-and-sister combinations as examples, and make each little boy feel that he must take care of his little partner. She can seat the children together in groups without regard for sex. She can stress the companionship of boys and girls in stories read by the group. She can encourage them to play together in mixed teams rather than having teams of either all boys or all girls to compete with each other.

In the upper elementary grades, where there are many early-maturing, over age Mexican children, this problem sometimes becomes very acute. The teacher must do all she can to promote the American attitude of wholesome accompanionship between the sexes in both work and play.

Combat the individualistic trait. This trait is brought out plainly in the history of Mexico that shows a rapid succession of rulers--individuals working for individual gain--who rose entirely through their own efforts without any sort of political party help or influence. It manifests itself, too, in the lack of cooperative enterprises or even pasttimes indluged in by the Mexican people.

Mexican boys and girls seem to have no conception of teamwork as understood by American youngsters fed on football, baseball, "the North," "the South," the Democrats, and the Republicans, all carrying with them the idea of cooperation. Therefore, the teacher must try to develop in them this feeling. One way is by organizing teams that can keep their identity over long periods of time, and that can play for the glory of their own group or their school. Along with this she can build up school or team spirit and develop loyal supporters who are willing to work with their chosen sides. In this work the teacher will note a strong Mexican trait, a tendency to "show off"--another manifestation of individualism--cropping out. She will have to subdue this desire for personal glory by isolating the offender, taking his name from the chart, listing him as a "poor sport" who breaks some of the rules the group has drawn for sportsmanship such as, "Work for the good of the team," and "Always cooperate," or by pointing out his offense and allowing group disapproval to fall heavily upon his head.

She can show the value of cooperation in other endeavors than games by promoting much group work in which each member is expected to contribute his share, and by organizing clubs for constructive work, or encouraging membership in such associations as Boy Scouts, or Campfire Girls. All such organizations emphasize mass effort rather than individual distinction.

Overcome the tendency to procrastinate. Mexico has long been known to Americans as "Manana-land" (wait-awhile), and "poco tiempo" (by and by), are common in their language. Even the very pictures that adorn many of the objects made in Mexico suggest this undesirable trait. For example, a common Mexican scene is that of an "hombre" drowsing against a wall or a tree with his chin resting on drawn-up knees and his whole body being shaded by his huge "sombrero" pulled low over his eyes. Such sights are common on the streets of towns in Mexico and in the "little Mexicos" of the United States. The general idea seems to be, "Never do today what you can put off until tomorrow."

The teacher can overcome this tendency by seeing that her Mexican children complete each day certain tasks that are set up in the morning. She must encourage them to perform certain duties on time. For example, she can budget the day's time and reward those who complete their work with a library reading period or free play time, while the others must work until finished.

One teacher, in order to overcome this trait of procrastination, devised a large weekly calendar of scheduled events and listed certain obligations the children must meet on time. With no further prompting or reminding from anyone, the children were to meet their obligations. If they did so, they were rewarded with a star on a chart; if not, a black cross was put beside their name. In addition, they were graded on the quality of their work. Of course, all strove to do the work well and on time in order to earn the bright-colored star rewards.

Thus, in these and many other ways, do the school teachers try to supply the training that they know is neglected in the Mexican homes, and endeavor to mold their little Mexican pupils into worthwhile citizens of America.

FOOTNOTE

[1]Wallace Thompson, The Mexican Mind: A Study of National Psychology (Boston: Little, Brown and Co., 1922), p. 91.

CHAPTER VII

HOW TO ESTABLISH A FEELING OF EQUALITY

One of the greatest problems facing the teacher of Mexican children is, how to develop and establish in these children a feeling of social equality with other races, particularly the Americans, who surround them. They must be given a basis of self-confidence, a certainty of their own abilities, and must be taught tolerance and some understanding in order that they may cope with the unfavorable attitudes they unfortunately will meet in their contacts with Americans.

It is a well-known fact that Americans possess a deep-rooted feeling of superiority toward other races, particularly toward those whose skins are dark. One authority, in referring to this attitude of Americans toward Mexicans, writes, "America has no technique for handling colored, or partly colored, persons as anything but a subordinated or isolated group."[1] This superior feeling toward Mexicans has manifested itself in many ways. Life among Americans, to the Mexican immigrant, has meant hardly more than a hopeless, blind struggle for existence. He is faced with the most unfavorable housing conditions; he is herded about in droves to satisfy the American desire for cheap labor; he comes in contact with snobbishness at every turn; and he is carelessly trod upon as though he were not a full-fledged human being or a potential citizen of the nation. In short, he is a victim of deplorable conditions which lead to mental conflicts and inferiority complexes. All this results in attitudes ranging from apparent acquiescence to bitter resentment; and, of course, all this is reflected in the Mexican children with which the teacher in the school must deal. It then becomes the teacher's duty to provide experiences in which socially desirable attitudes may be developed. If the child is to succeed in life, he must be provided with these very necessary tools of social adjustment.

I. BUILD SELF-CONFIDENCE

The feeling of social equality, like character, must be "caught;" it cannot be taught. It must be created through self-confidence. To be a successful guide in exposing her Mexican children to this happy feeling, the teacher must know that such an attitude is not gained by intellectual reasoning, but by emotions and experiences. She must, then, never lose sight of this goal in her teaching, the development of this feeling of equality. This must be done with enough subtlety that the children are never made conscious of it.

Some suggested means that the teacher can employ in her everyday contacts with the Mexican children to bring this about are given below.

Show no discrimination between American and Mexican children. Be quick to mete out the same punishment to American as Mexican or to reward each with the same privileges. When the Mexican children see that no difference is made in the treatment of members of their race and Americans, they will gain the feeling that they are of equal importance. For so many centuries the Mexican people have been downtrodden and oppressed. This has almost destroyed their sense of individuality and their self-respect. The teacher, through impartial, fair treatment of all in her group, can do much to restore this.

Create an informal teacher-pupil relationship. Give the Mexican child confidence in himself by making it easy for him to approach his teacher and talk with her on an equal basis with Americans.

Group lessons are one way of establishing this informal atmosphere. Instead of the formal rows of children in front of her, the teacher can gather them about her, perhaps in small chairs, on mats on the floor, or on the ground under some shade tree. In this way each child can be favored with the "personal touch," literally and figuratively speaking. This will help the Mexican child to gain a sense of his own importance as an individual.

Another device is to have a "cozy corner" in the room equipped with chairs or stools, possibly made from orange crates by the children themselves. A small rug on the floor, plants in pots, and other such equipment will give the Mexican children the sense of living in a homelike atmosphere. The teacher appears less formidable to the timid Mexican children when approached in such a setting.

The teacher may establish friendly relations with her Mexican children by mingling with them on the playground and entering into their play. The natural awe of "la maestra" felt by Mexican children can be made to disappear when she joins them in play.

One teacher of the writer's acquaintance was exceptionally successful in creating this desirable teacher-pupil relationsh with her Mexican children. One device she used was that of never failing to refer to them--in their presence or out --as "my young friends" or "our friends," and she always followed this up by treating them in just that way. This gave them a definite feeling of security and equality.

Encourage all attempts to use English. Miss Lucy Claire Hoard of El Paso, an authority on Mexican school children, believes that this is one of the surest ways of helping a Mexican child to gain a feeling of equality with American children. In order to feel equal, he must be able to employ the vital language tool as skillfully, and in order to do this, he must not be afraid to practice.

Children as a whole are naturally tactless and unintentionally cruel in their ridicule of those who make mistakes. Mexican children are praticularly sensitive to this when they make mistakes in the use of English. The teacher must set the example of infinite patience and kindness. She must teach the whole class that each should help the other in their efforts to express themselves.

Suppressing this tendency toward ridicule on the part of Americans of the group was handled rather cleverly and successfully in one school. The American children in the group, most of whom it seems had had some instruction in Spanish, were required to express themselves entirely in Spanish for a whole day. They immediately became conscious of the difficulty under which their Mexican comrades labored. The Mexicans became aware that they were equal to Americans, even surpassing them, when the overwhelming handicap of language was removed.

Special drills in various phases of language can be provided for the Mexican children, so that they may gain the desired skills, and with them, the needed confidence.

Though accuracy in the use of English is to be desired, caution must be exercised in correcting too often. Too frequent corrections will tend to destroy the very confidence the teacher is endeavoring to build up in the Mexican child's use of English.

Display an interest in members of the Mexican child's family. Mexican children delight in telling of the triumphs of some "beeg brother" or "seester," either in a higher school or in the community. The teacher can then use this as an example to suggest the quality of the Mexicans with other races.

Avoid such terms as "foreigner," "white child," and "American." These terms are sometimes used in this writing when the meaning is obvious, but they should not be employed in the schoolroom. They carry with them unpleasant implications to a mixed group. Only too well does the Mexican child realize he is a "foreigner" and that his skin is dark. More tactful terms that do not differentiate the groups must be employed if the Mexican is to be made to feel he is no different from the rest of the class.

In this connection it may be mentioned that though segregation is unlawful, accidents of residence sometimes cause almost one hundred percent Mexican enrollment in many schools. These children must be taught that this is not planned just because they are of a different race, that they are not considered "foreigners," but are white and American and are therefore being given the same advantages as others.

Put Mexican children in positions of trust. Allow them to be monitors, leaders, messengers, and teacher-helpers. When they see that they are worthy of the same trusts as the Americans of the group, they will feel that their positions are more nearly equal.

With this procedure the teacher can help those poor misfits, the overage, grade-retarded Mexican children who are so numerous in every school enrolling Mexicans. In the writer's high third grade of thirty-four children last year, the ages of a mixed group ranged from nine to fifteen years and the sizes were correspondingly different.

These large, overage children especially need to be made less conscious of their unfortunate position. The teacher can use these children as leaders in certain activities in which American and Mexican alike must follow. This will tend to give them the self-confidence and feeling of equality they so sorely need.

Let Mexicans compete with Americans when abilities are equal. Avoid unequal competitions. In several academic subjects, such as arithmetic and spelling, the Mexicans can compete on equal footing with Americans. Such contests will bring to the Mexican children a feeling that they are as intelligent as their English-speaking classmates. Even in subjects requiring a greater command of English, some of the Mexicans can hold their own, though defeat here sometimes has a serious effect because some of the Mexicans in the group are sure to feel the contest was unfair because of the language handicap. These contents should be arranged so that no thought of race will enter the children's minds; they must be thought of as contests of recognized abilities.

Miss Hoard stressed the fact that Mexicans are particularly adept at hand work of all kinds; penmanship, drawing, color work, clay-modeling, weaving, and construction with tools. The teacher can use these abilities to build in the child a recognition of his worth as a contributing member of society, as truly as are his American friends.

Build in the Mexicans a pride in their race. The teacher can show her group that the Mexican race has much to be proud of and much to contribute to the world. When this is felt, the Mexicans will more truly feel their equality with Americans.

The teacher may point out the beauties of the language, the picturesqueness of the country with its quaint villages, odd modes of travel, colorful costumes, interesting customs and games, and vivacious, lilting music. She may show how many of these contributions have been seized upon by the people of the United States. Mexican food, pottery, music, and architecture are all in common use, especially near the border.

The Mexican children will eagerly explain and demonstrate many of the above contributions. In this way, they gain a firm realization of their equality with Americans.

Set conduct patterns that will guide the Mexican children in their contacts with the community. This can be done through activities. Because of limited experiences and lack of home training, the Mexican children do not know how to conduct themselves in approved fashion in public. The teacher must enrich this meagre background with activities that will attain the desired results. Mexicans cannot feel equal in mingling with Americans unless they understand and can do the common things the Americans do.

Only when they feel sure of themselves will they be encouraged to stray from their "Little Mexico" homes and seek a place in American society.

II. TEACH TOLERANCE AND UNDERSTANDING

As the Mexican children grow older, they will become conscious of the fact that even though they believe in themselves and their own abilities, the Americans in the community do not display much faith in them or much tolerance toward them. This is not true in every community, but is so in far too many of them.

This lack of acceptance of Mexicans by Americans is being overcome to some extent in schools where both groups are represented, but the acute need for teaching this feeling of tolerance to Americans in other schools is not felt and, therefore, often not stressed.

This means that the teacher of Mexican children must give them some means of combatting the unfavorable American attitude. She must teach them tolerance and understanding in order to strengthen in the child the feeling of equality she has already so carefully established through building self-confidence in him during his earlier years in school. The methods suggested here will help to do this.

Discuss many racial groups. Mexican children may be shown in this way that their race is only one of many that contribute citizens to the United States, that theirs is not a unique position, but that they are equal with the rest of the many races and their contributions. Mexicans and Americans alike will come to have a mutual admiration and understanding of the other's worth.

The children may be made keenly aware of other nationalities through the study of current events. Some fine lessons in the value of tolerance and understanding can be drawn from the world events at the present time.

Analyze personal experiences of races represented in the group. Some of these experiences will be pleasant ones and some will be quite the opposite. The teacher must help the children to analyze these experiences and to understand that it is the ignorant or the thoughtless person who treats a member of another race as an inferior. Mexican children profit much by such discussions.

Provide for pleasurable contacts with Americans. The teacher must be sure of her ground here if she wishes to strengthen the feeling of equality in her Mexican children. She must arrange only those contacts in which she can be sure the Americans will receive the Mexicans favorably. In one situation, a ball game was arranged between two schools, and when the groups met, the Americans greeted and continually addressed the members of the Mexican team as "dirty greaser," "chili," and other insulting terms.

This clearly illustrates the necessity of teaching the Mexican children the attitude of tolerance as a means toward the feeling of equality and as a means of combatting this all too common American attitude.

Encourage participation in community activities and celebrations. In participating with Americans, the Mexicans will come to feel that they are a part of the group and no different from the rest. The teacher, even though she has children from the poorest of Mexican homes, should urge such participations as contributions to Red Cross drives or Community Chest funds, and attendance at community celebrations such as parades or picnics. These things will give the Mexican children a sense of "belonging."

Recognize Mexico as a "sister republic." Display the Mexican flag and Mexican articles in the room along with the American. Recognize Mexican holidays as well as American. Discuss the deeds of heroes of both nations. Through these procedures, the teacher sets the example of tolerance, understanding, and admiration for the Mexican nation and its people. The children in this atmosphere cannot help gaining a feeling of equality.

Develop an admiration for America as a nation. One way of stimulating this is by appealing to the emotions and love of ritual of the Mexican people through patriotic exercises, flag salutes, stirring patriotic songs and poems. The Mexicans will experience a feeling of pride and joy in the thought that they are part of this great nation, and that they can contribute toward its growth.

Stress to Mexicans their value as members of that race. The Mexicans must be made to see that they are not being urged to lose their racial identity, but that they are valued for it. Mexicans keenly resent the thought that they are being forced to desert their race to become American citizens. Show them that their ways, though different, are just as good as the American ways in many instances. This will enable them to attain the feeling of equality so necessary to their happiness and well-being in American society.

FOOTNOTE

[1] Max S. Handman, "The Mexican Immigrant in Texas," Proceedings of the National Conference of Social Work, (Cleveland, 1920), p. 336.

CHAPTER VIII

HOW TO MEET THE NEEDS OF MEXICAN BOYS AND GIRLS

AT UPPER ELEMENTARY LEVELS

Mexican boys and girls at the upper elementary levels present very definite problems to their teachers. In this sensitive period of adolescence, they need more than ever to be understood and to be guided skillfully through the handicaps which seem so overwhelming.

The children are usually overage, some two or three years. Their parents, having no precedent of lengthy education before them, seem to have the attitude that they, especially the girls, are getting too big to be idling away their time in school. They are needed to swell the meagre family income or to help at home with the work. The Mexican idea is that girls do not need much education; that their purpose in life is to become wives and mothers, so their place is in the home preparing for their future. It is expected that at an early age, thirteen or fourteen if not before, the boys will have gained sufficient knowledge to be able to carry on in some occupation, either as helpers to their fathers or as apprentices in some trade.

Of course, this parental attitude and lack of encouragement, together with the actual economic state so common among the Mexicans makes it difficult to interest the children and keep them in regular attendance in order that they may have the guidance so necessary to their welfare at this time.

The children, especially if they are members of a mixed group with Americans, feel very keenly their position. They lack a wholesome home environment that would give them the proper training in manners, dress, and pleasure activities. They may love their school and their teachers, but their parents are unsympathetic because they have no background for understanding the American schools. The children, under the parents' influence, feel the need of learning occupational skills and homemaking arts. In addition, they sense the difference between themselves and Americans and are very much in need of guidance in wholesome social living.

Here, then, are three worthy goals toward which the teachers of upper elementary Mexican children may strive. They may pursue means to interest the parents in schooling for the older boys and girls, and so hold them in school in order that they may receive some training in manual arts and homemaking, and some direction in how to live wholesomely. Of course, this is a big order, but teachers of Mexican children must understand the needs of these boys and girls and try to meet them in their classrooms.

I. ENLIST THE PARENTS' COOPERATION

A very great factor to be considered and dealt with in the education of Mexican children is their parents' attitudes toward schooling. In order to understand some of these attitudes which seem so foreign to American notions, the teacher must know something of the parents' educational background.

In Mexico, especially the Mexico of the parents' day, schooling was of a very formal sort. Much factual knowledge was crowded into little heads, and children were expected to parrot answer glibly though they had no understanding of the meanings. Contests were held frequently, and the fathers and mothers gathered to hear their offspring display learning and to see the most studious ones awarded medals for their feats of memory.

Coeducation had no part in the scheme of things as it was considered highly improper and undesirable to mix the sexes because of the detrimental effect on both academic progress and the moral development of the child.

In this formal school set-up, discipline was very strict, and punishments were often attended by public shame. One favorite form was to fasten paper donkey ears to the child's head and have him kneel in a window where passers-by and his schoolmates might see and laugh at him.

In such schools no place was found for play. The children were there to store up knowledge and they were supposed to come out, the boys at thirteen or fourteen--the girls earlier, ready for their life work as wage-earners or as wives and mothers.

These ideas of education differ so from American theories which see the child's development in terms of individual ability and personality as being far more important than more mastery of subject matter.

Teachers of Mexican children will find much truth and guidance in the following statement by Lyon, who says,

> The aims of the school are greatly magnified when it deals with a foreign group. The school has to go back a generation to the parents, and instill in them new attitudes and ideas concerning education.[1]

Ways to achieve these aims follow.

Encourage the parents to visit the school. Many of them will not willingly contact the schools for obvious reasons. They must be coaxed there with such lures as school entertainments. One good plan is to have a Fathers' or Mothers' Visiting Hour, and run through the day's work in ten- or fifteen-minute periods. Explanations should be made in Spanish if the parents are unable to comprehend English.

Another plan is to have auditorium programs which celebrate Mexican as well as American special occasions. Dramatizations from the history of both nations have proved of great value in cementing the feeling of mutual interest in several communities.

The teacher must take care to make the parents very welcome and must try to lessen their feelings of embarrassment and inferiority because of their ignorance and their poor clothes. She must encourage their attempts at English and if possible, use what words of Spanish she commands. Questions to them about Mexico, its customs, and its products, will help to put them at ease, will strengthen their self-assurance, and will show them that the school values what they and their children as Mexicans can contribute to American culture.

Through these visits and contacts the parents can be shown the worth of the schools to their children.

Explain conflicting ideas of American and Mexican education. In order to narrow the chasm of misunderstanding between American and Mexican ideas of education, the teacher must try to explain and demonstrate the advantages of such practices as coeducation, the activity method, play in school, informality, and the shift of emphasis from subject matter to child.

She must do this by enticing the parents to the school, then displaying to them through dramatizations and class activities that the older boys and girls have learned to work together as comrades with little thought of the other sex, that the activity method and play bring to them a vital interest and enthusiasm and at the same time make them learners, and that informality makes the child less conscious of himself and gives him more freedom to develop his own abilities.

Some parents will contact the school only on a summons to straighten out some disciplinary point. The teacher must seize this opportunity to drive in one of her explanatory wedges and try to make them understand the principles under which she works.

See that the parents understand explanations. Many of the Mexicans are so ignorant and have such a poor command even of their own language that explanations to them are very difficult. The teacher must see to it that the ideas are couched in language simple enough for them to understand. In most cases the children serve as interpreters and must be made to understand clearly what they are to tell so that further confusion will not be the result.

Often it is wise to send home explanations of acts that would be perfectly clear to American parents. For example, a bus excursion was planned with one group of Mexican children. The teacher did not think to tell them the details of the plan, and the next day over half the group came with the announcement, "My father say I cannot go." After a little questioning, the teacher realized that the fathers did not understand the purpose of the trip or that the children would be safely conducted by two teachers. A short explanatory note was prepared in both

English and Spanish and permission was then readily given. Some parents even gave brothers and sisters in other grades bus fare in the hope that they, too, would be allowed to go.

Display the children's accomplishments. Parents must be convinced that their children are learning what they think is important; namely, the English language, the use of tools, a mastery of factual subject matter, and homemaking arts. Frequent displays of these accomplishments will prove to the parents that the schools can train their boys to be more than just bootblacks, newsies, and messengers, and their girls to be efficient homemakers who are capable of bettering the deplorable conditions under which so many of them live.

Such displays can be made in the schools at entertainments and visiting-day programs.

Send materials into the homes. Many parents are too timid to be coaxed into the schools, no matter how alluring the bait, and many others are too tied down with work to spare time. These must be reached by sending into the homes the work of the schools.

The teacher must encourage the children to display their English, to teach it to their parents and others at home, and to read it to them whenever possible. She can send magazines, newspapers, lesson sheets, and booklets made by the children as carriers of English and of new ideas.

She can help the boys and girls to make all kinds of useful and decorative articles to brighten their drab home surroundings. She can plan with each child some improvement to be made in the home that will lighten a particular part of the parent's load, and help him to find ways of carrying it out.

All such activities will serve to interest the parents in the schools and show them that the time spent there by the children is very worthwhile.

II. GIVE OCCUPATIONAL AND HOMEMAKING TRAINING

The American's and the Mexican's ideas of length of education are very different. The American expects his children to enter a trade or profession after high school or college; the Mexican expects his to be ready much earlier.

Most public schools which the Mexicans attend are not designed for their special needs, but the teachers must do what they can to give these children some occupational and homemaking training before they are forced to drop their schooling. Some foresight as to their probable future in America suggests that such training is far more useful than the purely academic curricula designed for American elementary children.

Suggested procedures follow.

Have a gardening project. This is possible in a great many school situations. The children can study soils, seeds, and seasons. They can learn to cultivate the crops properly and care for the produce. This might be sold or sent into the homes. Out of this might come a useful study of food canning and preserving for the girls.

In one school visited, no plot of ground was available, but the children had built a number of boxes and had planted flowers in them. The study of soils, seeds, and seasons was part of this project, too, and the flowers were made into pretty bouquets and sold.

Such projects will give the children definite ways to earn money and this is so important to them.

Do much construction work. Both boys and girls can be taught to make many ornamental and useful things in the classroom. In many units of work, the construction of colonial coaches, viking ships, and airplanes, or rug- and basket-weaving, curtain-making, and costume-designing give the Mexican children much opportunity to handle tool and needle with facility. In addition, they learn to measure and to plan so as to conserve material, and to utilize things at hand for various purposes--valuable lessons all.

Instruct in how to work for other people. Studies in how to apply for positions are very profitable for Mexican children. The teacher can often secure various types of application blanks for positions and study them with the children. She can list points such as appearance, manners, and command of English, together with special requisites for certain positions, and help the children to prepare themselves along those lines.

Another important way of applying is by letter. This can be cared for in written composition classes and the importance of such points as form, clearness, and conciseness can be stressed.

It is surprising how ignorant many of the Mexican children are about telephones, transportation systems, and street maps. Such knowledges are very necessary in many of the jobs they will find to do, so the teacher can help them a great deal by incorporating such studies in the daily work.

Many of the girls will very likely find employment as house-servants. They should be taught something about cleaning, table-setting, and serving. Many teachers accomplish the first by directing girls as monitors who care for the room. One teacher took care of the latter two by teaching through pretended or real entertainments in which the children set the table with paper dishes, knives, and forks, as real ones were not available.

In another elementary school with a cafeteria, the Mexican children in the upper grades frequently had their lunch served semi-formally by the girls in the group.

Teach how to buy and sell. A fact often overlooked by those not familiar with the Mexicans, particularly the poor class, is that the children have practically no conception of money, especially sums greater than twenty-five or fifty cents. Therefore, lessons in values and in making change are very helpful to them. Even though these children are rather old for a play store, at least one teacher found it successful by setting up a model of a prosperous little food store in the neighborhood. The families of many of the boys and girls in the class traded there and each day their purchases were duplicated in class. A box of play money, very realistic in appearance, and a paste-board cash register made by the boys added much to the study. The class and the teacher analyzed together needs of each family and the purchases made. Ways were sought to improve upon the latter. The children learned the advantages of quantity and quality buying and how the perishables could be guarded from decay. The handling of money was taught, too. Later in the term, a credit system was established and the children learned much valuable information about business in this play store.

In another school the fifth grade Mexican class each term buys candy at wholesale and sells it at retail prices to the children of the school. The knowledge gained is of great worth to them, and the use of profits made over a period of several years has carried with it some fine lessons in wise buying.

Have studies of activities in the home. Many topics concerning home activities which are a matter of course to American children must be taught to the Mexican whose ignorance and lack of background makes them unknown to him.

In one Mexican school, at the beginning of the term, a large "Home Activities" wall chart was prepared. Columns were headed by such items as "Housecleaning," "Yards," "Home Nursing," "Pests," "Mosquito Congrol," "Preservation of Foods," and "Child Care." Time was devoted each day to a short discussion on one or two of the topics. Pertinent questions were formulated, written on slips of paper, and put into slits under the proper headings on the chart. Committees were appointed to seek answers to the questions and report on them at a future date. A large scrap book was divided into sections corresponding with the chart items, as were individual notebooks belonging to the children. The committeemen were encouraged to seek many sources for their answers and they interviewed people, searched the library, and sent off to magazines and to Government printing offices for pamphlets and household hints. After reports were made, the questions and their answers were recorded in the notebooks and in the proper section on the "Home Activities" scrap book. This book, containing much information of real value, was presented to the school library for use by future classes.

Such a plan was found to be very helpful to the Mexicans, as the questions were on their own particular problems, and the answers finally formed were what they themselves could do with the limited facilities at their command.

Make English of primary importance in all studies. The teacher must always keep in mind that language is the Mexican's greatest handicap and must design her procedures so that English is of primary importance in all activities.

Much dramatization and oral work are necessary with Mexican children. Activities in which the boys and girls must appear before outsiders and use English will help them to overcome their timidity and reluctancy to speak their acquired language and will give them the self-assurance they must have to mingle with Americans to seek work or worthy pleasure.

One way to make the children see the value of English is to have them make a study of types of employment and amount of wages among the people they know. In most communities it will be found that those who know English well command far better positions and pay then those who speak only Spanish or limited English.

This will encourage them to make the most of their opportunities to learn their second language well.

III. GUIDE IN WHOLESOME SOCIAL LIVING

Elsewhere in this writing it has been said that the parents of Mexican children must be made to understand the conflicting ideas of the schools of Mexico and of America. It is just as important that the children be helped to understand the conflict of ideas between Old Mexico and Young America. The teacher must realize that teaching these Mexican boys and girls means far more than merely teaching them the requirements of the grade; it means teaching them how to live as well.

As the children reach the upper elementary grades, they begin to feel very keenly the difference between their suppressed activities and the freedom which American boys and girls enjoy. This makes them go to extremes to try to obtain the same liberties, and in these extremes lie dangers.

A few suggestions as to how the teachers may start these Mexican boys and girls on the right paths toward wholesome living follow.

Make association between the sexes commonplace. Again the trait of sex-consciousness arises, more important at this age than ever before. The teacher must discuss frankly with the children their parents ideas of chaperonage and try to make them understand the fathers' and mothers' attitude in this matter. At the same time we must try to bring about a comradely association between the boys and girls.

This can be done by giving them work and play in which they mingle freely with no thought of the other sex. Creating positions which are filled equally well by boy or girl is one good way of bringing this about.

Another way is by grouping them together regardless of sex and building up among them a spirit of mutual helpfulness and cooperation in any task they might undertake, whether it be setting the room to rights after a busy day or winning a volleyball game.

Develop standards for pleasing personal appearance. One teacher guided the Mexican children's notions about appropriate clothing through a unit on fabrics which was an outgrowth of other units on the production of cotton, wool, and silk. Many pictures were studied, people were closely observed, and standards of dress for various occasions were drawn up for both goys and girls.

In connection with this study, the teacher included instruction on the wise use of cosmetics, nail polish, and hair oil. These were all vital topics with Mexican children, as they lack home guidance and often array themselves in the most "flashy" fashion. Mexican girls frequently create very bad impressions with gaudy, inappropriate clothes, brilliant nails, cheeks, and lips, a mass of very oily curls, cheap dangling earrings, and heavily-scented perfume. Boys were equally guilty with their thick black hair and long sideburns reeking of oil, and wide bell-bottom trousers in feeble imitation of a much more picturesque Spanish style.

The teacher must try to guide these children's tastes along more simple and cleanly lines through units of work, frank bits of advice, and by her own example of simple dress and immaculate grooming.

Organize many types of clubs. Many teachers questioned recommended clubs of all types as meeting definite needs in the lives of Mexican children. Among a people who naturally enjoy gathering together, clubs lend definite purposes to such gatherings.

In the classroom, instead of having only one or two clubs to which every one belongs, the teacher can allow several groups to form themselves according to their individual interest. The clubs may have as their purposes such activities as sewing, basket-weaving, and clay-modeling, or the study of some worthwhile subject such as aviation or radio.

One interesting club has as its purpose the discussion of practical questions that the children wanted answers to. A question box was provided and was opened at club meetings. Questions of public conduct, chaperonage, proper dress, and home problems were always found within, and in helping Mexican children to find answers, the motherly teacher was able to give them much valuable guidance they could not get in their homes.

Another teacher organized a combination reading and handwork club. Its membership was composed of present students of her grade and former ones who had not for some unfortunate reason been able to continue their schooling. Those on the program entertained by reading various types of material while the others carried on their sewing, painting, drawing, or modeling as they wished.

Such clubs as this just described can keep the boys and girls in touch with the English they have learned and can develop very worthwhile leisure time habits in many lives that are denied schooling too soon.

Overcome the tendency to shrink from contacts with Americans. By the time Mexican children reach the upper elementary grades, they are usually very shy and self-conscious, especially when mingling with Americans. The teacher can help them to overcome this and put them at ease by allowing them to be hosts at little social affairs. For example, the fifth grade Mexican children in one school of mixed enrollment always assumed charge of the visitors at any school affair and learned the common courtesies of greeting the visitors, learning their names, introducing them, conducting them about, explaining points of interest, and finding seats for them. They were very proud of this responsibility and always performed it willingly and well.

Another teacher stressed class activities that would bring the Mexican children in contact with Americans, the teachers in the school and the merchants in the neighborhood. One of these was a weekly newspaper, printed by hectograph. The children were expected to interview people and gather news and advertising for the weekly edition. The copies were eagerly awaited and were distributed in school and community with great pride.

Such activities bring about a better understanding and friendly feeling between American and Mexican and help to diminish the old racial prejudices that seem to exist in so many communities.

Study many leisure time activities. Unfortunately the Mexicans have few leisure time pursuits open to them which better class Americans consider worthy. The boys, imitating their elders, find pleasures in gambling, cockfights, pool rooms, and cheap dance halls. Many of the girls are so guarded that they must slip off and steal forbidden fruit or are so rebellious and unguided that they easily follow undesirable paths.

In order to help these children who are the strained links between old ideas and a new and changing world to find safe pleasures, the teacher must try to develop tastes and interests in a higher type of leisure.

One way is to establish in them very firmly the library habit. If this is not possible in the community, the teacher can probably gather good magazines and interest the children in them. In one town, the teacher of a Mexican school helped her sixth grade pupils to establish a used-magazine library service. The children wrote notes to those people in the community who were likely subscribers, explaining their aim, and met with splendid cooperation when they called at the homes where they were given dozens of old magazines. The magazine library was opened to the school first and later to the Mexican neighborhood whose residents, many of whom were ex-pupils of the school, came eagerly at library hour seeking suggestions for improvement of living conditions, for guidance in the pursuance of hobbies, and for fictional entertainment. One feature of this library was the helpful service given by the pupils who had studied with the teacher the contents of the magazines and had specialized in groups on certain features. This developed in them special interests which could be carried on outside the school.

Another way to guide these Mexican children to find safe pleasures is to interest the boys in American sports such as football and baseball, and the girls in dramatization, folk-dancing, and group singing. This work can easily be included in daily recreational periods.

Still another way to help them is to study with them the lives of outstanding world figures and to instill in their minds such worthy character traits as are displayed by real heroes in contrast to the gangsters and their molls whose lives seem so full of the thrill and excitement young hearts crave. This gangster wave is a real danger and the teacher must try to counteract it by helping her Mexican children to distinguish between worthy and unworthy conduct to imitate.

So it is that in these and many other ways can the teachers in their classrooms meet the problems which Mexican boys and girls present to the schools of America.

FOOTNOTE

[1] L. L. Lyon, "Investigation of the Program for the Adjustment of Mexican Girls to the High Schools of the San Fernando Valley," (Unpublished Master's thesis, University of Southern California, Los Angeles, 1933), p. 19.

BIBLIOGRAPHY

Armour, B. "Problems in the Education of the Mexican Child," The Texas Outlook, 16:29-31, December, 1932.

Bogardus, E. S. "The Mexican Immigrant and Segregation," American Journal of Sociology, 36:74-80, August, 1930.

_____. The Mexican in the United States, Los Angeles: University of Southern California Press, 1934, 126 pp.

Bowers, G. "Mexican Education in East Donna," The Texas Outlook, 15:29-30, March, 1931.

Branigan, J. "The Education of the Overage Mexican Child," Sierra Education News, 29:37-9, December, 1933.

Buckner, H. A. "A Study of Pupil Elimination and Failure Among Mexicans," Unpublished Masters Thesis, University of Southern California, Los Angeles, California, 1935, 159 pp.

Carpenter, C. C. "A Study of Segregation versus Non-segregation of Mexican Children." Unpublished Master's thesis, University of Southern California, Los Angeles, California, 1936, 157 pp.

Crawford, C. C., and E. M. Leitzell. Learning a New Language. Los Angeles: C. C. Crawford, University of Southern California, 1930, 242 pp.

Delmet, D. T. "A Study of the mental and Scholastic Abilities of Mexican Children in the Elementary School." Upublished Master's thesis, University of Southern California, Los Angeles, California, 1928, 106 pp.

Dickenson, R. E. "Some Suggestive Problems in the Americanization of Mexicans," Pedagogical Seminary, 26:288-97, September, 1919.

Foster, L. G. "Teaching Non-English Children," Sierra Educational News, 27:30-32, December, 1931.

Frank, Eva A. "The Mexican 'Just Won't Work,'" Nation, 125-155-7, August, 1927.

Gamio, Manuel. Mexican Immigration to the United States. Chicago: University of Chicago Press, 1930, 262 pp.

Gould, Betty, "Methods of Teaching Mexicans," Unpublished Master's thesis, University of Southern California, Los Angeles, California, 1932, 121 pp.

Handman, Max S. "The Mexican Immigrant in Texas," Proceedings of the National Conference of Social Work. Cleveland, 1920.

Hoard, L. C. Teaching English to the Spanish-Speaking Child in the Primary Grades. El Paso, Texas: El Paso Public Schools, 1936, 108 pp.

Holliday, J. M. "A Study of non-Attendance in Miguel Hidalgo School of Brawley, California," Unpublished Master's thesis, University of Southern California, Los Angeles, California, 1936, 77 pp.

Lanigan, Mary. "Second Generation Mexicans in Belvedere." Unpublished Master's thesis, University of Southern California, Los Angeles, California, 1932, 86 pp.

Leis, W. W. "The States of Education for Mexican Children in Four Border States." Unpublished Master's thesis, University of Southern California, Los Angeles, California, 1932, 78 pp.

Lyon, L. L. "Investigation of the Program for the Adjustment of Mexican Girls to the High Schools of the San Fernando Valley," Unpublished Master's thesis, University of Southern California, Los Angeles, California, 1933, 74 pp.

McCammon, E. L. "A Study of Children's Attitudes Toward Mexicans." California Journal of Elementary Education, 5:119-28, November, 1936.

Manuel, H. T. The Education of the Mexican and Spanish-Speaking Children in Texas. The Fund for Research in the Social Sciences. Austin: The University of Texas, 1930, 173 pp.

_____. "The Spanish-Speaking Child," The Texas Outlook, 14:21, January, 1930.

Martindale, G. "Teaching English to Mexican Boys," Elementary English Review, 6:276-8, December, 1929.

Neal, E. A. "Adapting the Curriculum to Non-English-Speaking Children." Elementary English Review, 6:183-5, September, 1929.

_____ and Ollie P. Storm. "Teachers' Manual," for The Open Door Primer. New York: The Macmillan Co., 1927.

Reynolds, Annie. "The Education of Spanish-Speaking Children in Five Southwestern States," Buletin No. 11. Washington, D.C.: United States Government Printing Office, United States Department of the Interior, Office of Education, 1933, 64 pp.

Riddlebarger, Glenn. "A Real Activity Program" Sierra Educational News, 27: 42, June, 1931.

Rodee, Nona. Teaching Beginners to Speak English. Tucson, Arizona: Tucson Public Schools, 1923, 129 pp.

Schroff, Ruth. "A Study of Social Distance between Mexican Parents and American
T   Teachers in San Bernardino, California," Upublished Master's thesis, University of Southern California, Los Angeles, California, 1936, 108 pp.

Sixk, W. O. "Mexicans in the Texas Schools," The Texas Outlook, 14:10-12. December, 1930.

"Special Report on Foreign-born White Families by Country of Birth of Head," Fifteenth Census of the United States: 1930. Population. United States Department of Commerce. Bureau of the Census. Washington: United States Government Printing Office, 1933, 218 pp.

Stanley, Grace. "Special Schools for Mexicans," Survey, 44:714-15, September 15, 1920.

Thompson, Wallace. The Mexican Mind: A Study of National Psychology. Boston: Little, Brown and Co., 1922, 303 pp.

Treff, S. L. "The Education of Mexican Children in Orange County," Unpublished Master's thesis, University of Southern California, Los Angeles, California, 1934, 144 pp.

Walker, Helen. "The Conflict of Cultures in First Generation Mexicans in Santa Ana, California," Unpublished Master's thesis, University of Southern California, Los Angeles, California, 1928, pp. 99.

Weir, E.P., "The Mexican Child," The Texas Outlook, 20:23, June, 1936.

Wilder, Mrs. L. A. "Programs in the Teaching of Mexican Children," The Texas Outlook, 20:9-10, August, 1936.